P9-DXO-870

Fast and

Simple

DIABETES

MENUS

Betty Wedman–St. Louis, Ph.D., R.D., C.N.S.

New York Chicago San Francisco Lisbon London Madrid Mexico City
Milan New Delhi San Juan Seoul Singapore Sydney Toronto

The *McGraw·Hill* Companies

Library of Congress Cataloging-in-Publication Data

Wedman-St. Louis, Betty.
    Fast and simple diabetes menus / by Betty Wedman-St. Louis.— 1st ed.
        p.   cm.
    ISBN 0-07-142255-2
    1. Diabetes—Diet therapy—Recipes.   I. Title.

    RC662 .W364   2004
    641.5′6314—dc22   2003025063

Many thanks to the vision of Judith McCarthy, Senior Editor at McGraw-Hill, for giving me the opportunity to answer the requests of so many people with diabetes for menu and recipe tips for blood glucose management and other dietary disorders

Copyright © 2004 by Betty Wedman-St. Louis. All rights reserved. Printed in the United States of America. Except as permitted under the United States Copyright Act of 1976, no part of this publication may be reproduced or distributed in any form or by any means, or stored in a database or retrieval system, without the prior written permission of the publisher.

4 5 6 7 8 9 10 11 12 13 14 15 16 17 18 19   DOC/DOC   0 9 8 7

ISBN-13: 978-0-07-142255-0
ISBN-10:   0-07-142255-2

Interior design by Robert S. Tinnon Design

McGraw-Hill books are available at special quantity discounts to use as premiums and sales promotions, or for use in corporate training programs. For more information, please write to the Director of Special Sales, Professional Publishing, McGraw-Hill, Two Penn Plaza, New York, NY 10121-2298. Or contact your local bookstore.

This book is printed on acid-free paper.

To my beloved Chrissy, a silver Persian cat, who taught me how to

be a diabetes educator for someone who can't talk . . .

Contents

Chapter 3 Recipes   *43*

Appendix

Index   193

Preface

Americans have a new recipe for home cooking—fast, faster, and fastest! Today's cooks are marching back into the kitchen, demanding more creativity in menus and convenience from food suppliers. The menus and recipes in *Fast and Simple Diabetes Menus* are intended to fulfill that desire.

This book includes exciting new recipes for main dish salads like South of the Border Chicken Salad, accompaniments like Avocado Potato Salad, and breakfast items like Banana Split Muffin Sundae. Meal replacement bars may be OK in a pinch, but they leave a lot lacking psychologically. Put a bar on a dinner plate, and see how much your taste buds are excited.

Many recipes in *Fast and Simple Diabetes Menus* feature fresh herbs. Some people believe stashing basil will attract success and prosperity. Others believe sprinkling rosemary around their home will bring protection and good luck. These beliefs may or may not be true, but one thing is certain—these herbs can add fabulous flavor and aroma to your meals. Try the recipes in this book, and enjoy the unique flavor that herbs and spices can bring to your menu.

Bon appétit!

Introduction

According to the American Diabetes Association (ADA), over 17 million people in the United States have diabetes. More than 2,000 people are diagnosed with diabetes every day! Diabetes is a disorder that affects the body's ability to produce or respond to insulin. The body needs the hormone insulin to allow glucose to enter the cells, where it can be used for energy. If diabetes is left untreated or poorly treated, complications like heart disease, stroke, kidney failure, blindness, and nerve damage may result.

Nutrition Goals

There is no specific diet for people with diabetes. Instead, food and menu choices emphasize normalization of blood glucose levels. People with diabetes are often amazed when they hear a diabetes educator tell them they can eat any food in moderation—as long as they plan for the effect it will have on their blood sugar level. Since carbohydrate content has a major effect on blood glucose, the goal is to keep intake of carbohydrates as consistent as possible from day to day.

Another important dietary goal is to limit the amount of saturated fat in the diet. One of the complications of diabetes is an increased risk of heart disease. Saturated fats in fatty meats, whole-milk products and cheeses, and fried foods are best kept to a minimum to control hyperlipidemia, the presence of an abnormally high concentration of fats in the blood.

The best foods for a person with diabetes are the ones that are healthful choices for everyone else: vegetables, whole grains, fruits, low-fat dairy products, fish, and lean meats. Instead of struggling with what to serve with your chicken breast every night, look for inspiration from the menu choices in *Fast and Simple Diabetes Menus*. Then compare your options if you had lived two million years ago with today:

• **Hunter-gatherer diet**—In Paleolithic times, our ancestors ate what they could hunt and gather. The original human diet was lean meats, fish, nuts, seeds, nonstarchy vegetables and fruits, and occasionally honey. The hunter stalked his prey as the early rays of sun filtered through the trees. He quickly fitted an arrow to the bowstring, aimed, and shot. If he hit his mark, he would be glad to have food to eat. Women wandered far and wide to find berries, greens, tubers, and occasionally bird eggs for their contribution to the daily meal. Each day they had to collect firewood and herbs to ensure a tasty menu, as well as the warmth and protection of fire during the night.

• **Modern-day diet**—Today we eat a chocolate-covered doughnut for breakfast, open a can of spaghetti and meatballs for lunch, and have pizza delivered for dinner while watching television throughout the evening. Is there any doubt about why obesity is a major problem in our society?

Anyone with diabetes can achieve reasonable nutrition goals without feeling deprived. The menus and recipes in *Fast and Simple Diabetes Menus* are designed to help you achieve weight goals while maintaining good blood glucose control.

Carbohydrates and Sweeteners

The amount of carbohydrates will vary in each individual's meal plan, but current nutrition recommendations do not require that people with diabetes avoid simple sugars. The objective is to focus on *total* carbohydrates instead of the source of carbohydrates consumed. Eating fruits, milk, potatoes, rice, bread, and other carbohydrate sources in a consistent meal plan may be just as effective for blood glucose management as avoiding sucrose-containing foods. Recipes in this book use sucrose and sugar substitutes as sweeteners.

Fats

The recommended amount of fat in the diet is usually based on lipid management goals. People who are at a healthy weight and have normal lipid levels can consume more liberal amounts of fat than can those who need to lose weight, lower triglycerides, or follow very low-density lipoprotein modifications.

Limiting consumption of fried foods and fatty meats and dairy foods can help keep saturated fats in the diet to less than 10 percent of the daily calories.

Protein

There is insufficient evidence to support recommended protein intakes in the diet. Protein does become an important factor when nephropathy (kidney disease) complications are identified. When glomerulus filtration rate (GFR) begins to fall, protein intake should be reduced so the body can maintain kidney function as long as possible without compromising muscle strength.

Chapter 1
Diabetes and Complicating Factors

Diabetes and Hyperlipidemia

*I*n a 2002 study of cardiovascular disease and diabetes by the National Diabetes Education Program, over 60 percent of patients surveyed did not consider heart attacks or strokes to be a serious complication of the disease. The older the patients, the less likely they were to rate cardiovascular disease as a serious concern. Those surveyed rated blindness and amputations as more serious than premature death from a heart attack or stroke.

Yet diabetes can damage large and small blood vessels. Scars form inside the blood vessels, making the walls stiff and hard. These scarred places trap cholesterol and may eventually lead to a blocked vessel. When a blood vessel becomes blocked, the heart must work harder to pump blood through the obstructed vessel. Consequences may include heart attacks, strokes, high blood pressure, and poor blood circulation in the arms, legs, and head.

To combat the complications of cardiovascular disease, the National Cholesterol Education Program recommends that individuals limit their intake of foods with high fat content. Foods high in saturated fatty acids and trans fats can be replaced with unsaturated fatty acids from fish, vegetables, legumes, and nuts.

Since high-carbohydrate diets can increase triglycerides and lower high-density lipoprotein (HDL) cholesterol, whole grains and whole fruits are recommended instead of refined-carbohydrate sources.

After years of focusing on low-density lipoprotein (LDL) cholesterol as the "bad" fat in the blood, scientists are finally taking another look at triglycerides. Research shows that high triglycerides alone can raise the risk of cardiovascular disease. Triglycerides are the most common source of fat in the body. Some come from foods you eat. Others are made by the body. Too high a triglyceride level in the blood is called *hypertriglyceridemia*. New recommended government guidelines set the goal at 150 milligrams per deciliter after a twelve-hour (overnight) fast. If your triglyceride level exceeds this goal, lifestyle changes can help lower elevated triglycerides:

- Lose weight.
- Reduce your consumption of saturated fat and high-cholesterol foods.
- Drink less alcohol.
- Increase physical activity.
- Eat fatty fish (for example, tuna, mackerel, sardines, and salmon).

When most people think of heart disease or cardiovascular disease, they think of cholesterol levels in the blood. The levels of HDL and LDL cholesterol are important to monitor regularly. The National Cholesterol Education Program recommends the following levels:

HDL ("good") cholesterol	Greater than 45 mg/dl in men
	Greater than 55 mg/dl in women
LDL ("bad") cholesterol	Less than 100 mg/dl

If detected soon enough, hyperlipidemia, or a high concentration of fats in the blood, can usually be corrected by a healthful diet and exercise. To illustrate how dietary habits can influence hyperlipidemia, the table compares two days of menus. The high-cholesterol, high-fat menu from restaurant meals may be a "vacation treat" menu, but it does not fit the recommendations for a heart-healthy diet.

High-Cholesterol, High-Fat Menu: Restaurant Meals

Meal	Serving	Cholesterol (mg)	Total Fat (g)	Saturated Fat (g)
Breakfast				
Egg McMuffin	1	226	11	4
Orange juice	4 oz.	–	–	–
Milk, whole	8 oz.	34	8	5
TOTAL		260	19	9
Lunch				
Big Mac	1	103	32	10
Fries, regular	1	12	17	7
Milk, whole	8 oz.	34	8	5
Apple pie	1	12	15	5
TOTAL		161	72	27
Dinner				
Beef tenderloin	1	90	25	6
Fries, regular	1	12	17	7
Milk, whole	8 oz.	34	8	5
TOTAL		136	50	18
Total daily intake		557	141	54

Low-Cholesterol, Low-Fat Menu: Home Preparation

Meal	Serving	Cholesterol (mg)	Total Fat (g)	Saturated Fat (g)
Breakfast				
English muffin	1	–	–	–
Canadian bacon	1 oz.	25	3	1
Milk, skim	8 oz.	5	–	–
Tub margarine	2 tsp.	–	6	1
Orange juice	4 oz.	–	–	–
	TOTAL	30	9	2
Lunch				
Turkey	1 oz.	22	1	–
Bread	2 slices	–	–	–
Salad dressing	1 tsp.	1	2	–
Chips	½ c.	–	5	1
Zucchini cake	1 serving	–	5	1
Milk, skim	8 oz.	5	–	–
	TOTAL	28	13	2
Dinner				
Fish (salmon)	5 oz.	113	6	2
Mashed potatoes	½ c.	–	4	1
Corn	½ c.	–	4	1
Tossed salad	1 c.	–	–	–
Dressing	1 tbsp.	–	5	1
Tub margarine	1 tsp.	–	3	1
Sherbet	½ c.	–	–	–
Milk, skim	8 oz.	5	–	–
	TOTAL	118	22	6
Total daily intake		176	44	10

Diabetes and Hypertension

Hypertension, or high blood pressure, affects about fifty million
Americans (one in four adults), and a significant number of them

also have diabetes. The following guidelines define normal blood pressure and the levels of hypertension (systolic over diastolic pressure):

Blood Pressure Category	Systolic/Diastolic Measurement
Normal	Less than 120/less than 80 mm Hg
Prehypertension	120 to 139/80 to 89 mm Hg
Stage 1 hypertension	140 to 159/90 to 99 mm Hg
Stage 2 hypertension	160 or greater/100 or greater mm Hg

The treatment goal for hypertension is to lower blood pressure to less than 140 mm Hg systolic and less than 90 mm Hg diastolic. For those with diabetes and chronic kidney disease, the goal is stricter: less than 130 mm Hg systolic and less than 80 mm Hg diastolic.

In May 2003, the National Heart, Lung, and Blood Institute (NHLBI) released new guidelines advising Americans to make needed lifestyle changes—losing excess weight, increasing physical activity, following a heart-healthy diet—to reduce the damage caused by high blood pressure. Cutting back on salt and high-sodium foods in the diet may help manage prehypertension and/or reduce the amount of medication needed to control blood pressure.

The average American diet contains greater than 6,000 milligrams of sodium per day. More than 75 percent of that sodium comes from packaged and processed foods. Convenience foods tend to be high in sodium, so meal planning requires a rethinking of food choices.

A healthful diet usually contains 2,500 to 3,000 milligrams of sodium per day. For comparison, consider that one teaspoon of salt has about 2,400 milligrams of sodium. The obvious way to reduce sodium content is to avoid using table salt. Less obvious sources of sodium include the following foods:

- **Seasonings and condiments**—Soy sauce, garlic salt, onion salt, bouillon, olives, pickles, relishes
- **Dairy products**—Processed cheese, cheese spreads, buttermilk
- **Soups**—Bouillon cubes; canned, dried, or frozen soup mixes; canned broths
- **Vegetables**—Frozen vegetables with prepared sauces, sauerkraut
- **Meat and fish**—Canned, cured, dried, salted, or smoked meats and fish, bacon, hot dogs, ham, corned beef, luncheon meats, sausage, canned tuna
- **Fast foods**—Pizza, Chinese foods (unless they are prepared without MSG, soy sauce, oyster sauce, etc.), deluxe hamburgers
- **Cereals and breads**—Instant mixes such as those for biscuits, muffins, and quick breads
- **Convenience items**—Packaged sauces, including spaghetti sauce, au jus and gravies, seasoned pasta and rice, stuffing mixes
- **Snack foods**—Corn chips, potato chips, pretzels, party dips and spreads

Spices and herbs can provide flavor and enhance meal choices. The recipes in *Fast and Simple Diabetes Menus* feature many commonly available fresh herbs and spices found in the local supermarket. A lower-sodium diet does *not* have to be bland and tasteless.

Diabetes and Kidney Disease

Diabetes is a leading cause of kidney failure. Over thirteen million people with diabetes are at risk for developing kidney disease. It often goes unrecognized, underdiagnosed, and undertreated until too late. The progression of proteinuria—spilling of protein in the urine—may develop slowly over the years.

Early in the development of kidney disease, the kidneys begin working less efficiently in removing waste products from the blood. Proteins are then lost in the urine instead of being used for cell repair and growth. As the disease progresses, kidneys lose their ability to remove creatinine and urea (waste products) from the blood. Kidney disease is a silent disease complication of diabetes, so each person needs to be familiar with the four stages of the disorder:

• **Stage 1**—Blood flow through the kidneys remains normal or near normal, but the glomeruli (the "filter paper") begin to show damage. Tears or leaks in the glomeruli allow small amounts of protein, called albumin, to leak into the urine. Your physician may refer to this as micro albuminuria, which is said to be present if urinary albumin excretion is 30 milligrams to 299 milligrams per 24 hours (or 20 micrograms to 199 micrograms per minute on a timed specimen or 30 milligrams per gram creatinine to 299 milligrams per gram creatinine on a random specimen). People with diabetes may live with small amounts of albumin loss for years if their blood glucose and blood pressure are well controlled.

• **Stage 2**—The loss of albumin plus other proteins in the urine becomes greater than the amounts in Stage 1 for micro albuminuria. Blood levels of creatinine and BUN (blood urea nitrogen) begin to rise, indicating the kidneys' loss of filtering ability.

• **Stage 3**—The glomeruli of the kidneys become even less able to filter out waste products. Large amounts of protein are lost in the urine. Blood pressure usually increases significantly. Higher levels of creatinine are found in the blood.

• **Stage 4**—End-stage renal disease (ESRD) is diagnosed when the glomerular filtration rate drops so low that dialysis is needed to remove waste products from the blood. Urine output declines and frequently ceases.

Functioning kidneys are critical to survival. They contain a complex filter that allows water to pass through but traps protein. The protein is needed for cell repair and growth. High blood sugar and high blood pressure are toxic to the complex filter in the kidneys. You should take the following actions to minimize damage to the kidneys:

• **Control your blood pressure**—Hypertension (high blood pressure) is a major factor in the onset of kidney dysfunction. When blood pressure exceeds 140/90 mm Hg, doctors usually prescribe an ACE (angiotensin-converting enzyme) inhibitor medication.

• **Evaluate each new medicine very carefully**—Every day seems to bring another story from a patient who says, "Starting on a new medication caused me to be on dialysis." Not everyone detoxifies a drug in the same way. Anti-inflammatory drugs seem to be major culprits for kidney disregulation, followed closely by antibiotics. Whenever you add any new drugs to your regimen, get a blood and/or urine assessment. It may help save your kidney cells from destruction.

• **Reduce the protein in your diet**—As soon as micro albuminuria and/or elevated creatinine values are detected, start spacing the protein in your diet into three or four meals. A scrambled egg at breakfast, a 2-ounce ground-beef patty for lunch, and 2 ounces (2 legs) of chicken at dinner would be a good start.

• **Have your urine tested annually for micro albuminuria**—The urinary albumin-to-creatinine ratio is best measured in an early morning urine sample. I predict that, in the near future, individuals with diabetes will test their own micro albuminuria to assess their tolerance level for dietary protein. That will let us really tailor meal plans to the individual! Micro albuminuria rarely occurs before puberty, so for those with type 1 diabetes, testing should start then and be repeated five years later. Because of the difficulty in assessing the precise onset of type 2 diabetes, testing for individuals with type 2 needs to be done at the time of diagnosis and repeated annually.

• **Check your hemoglobin A1C every three months**—Balancing diet, medication, and exercise to maintain normal blood glucose levels as often as possible may help reduce your risk of kidney dysfunction. An elevated A1C means that an abnormal amount of glycoproteins is causing the thickening of the glomeruli membranes. This thickening reduces blood flow and produces the loss of filtering ability.

Diet Management

When kidney dysfunction is first diagnosed, a 60-gram protein diet is recommended to reduce damage to the glomeruli. A major nutrition goal is to keep protein portions small at each meal. The diet seldom limits sodium, phosphorus, and potassium unless blood tests indicate a need. Beverages consumed with these meals should contain no protein. If extra calories are needed to maintain weight, French bread and margarine or butter can be added to the meals suggested in the table.

As kidney cells become too damaged to filter out excess sodium, potassium, and waste products from metabolism, dialysis is needed either temporarily or as a life support. Because of the albumin lost in the dialysis "kidney," a person at this stage may need a higher level of protein in the diet. Restrictions on foods that are high in potassium, sodium, and phosphorus make menu planning very challenging. The 80-gram protein diet in the table provides an example of how to manage these restrictions. If extra calories are needed to maintain weight, slices of French bread with margarine or butter can be added to meals.

Sample 60-Gram Protein Diet

Breakfast	Lunch	Dinner
Day 1		
½ cup apple juice	2-ounce ground beef	2 ounces Lemon-Garlic
1 egg, scrambled	patty	Cornish Hens (see page 101)
2 slices French bread,	1 hamburger bun	1 cup steamed rice
toasted	Ketchup, onion, lettuce	½ cup green peas
1 tablespoon margarine	1 fresh pear	½ cup cole slaw with carrots
or butter	5 vanilla wafers	1 slice angel food cake
Low-sugar jelly	Beverage	½ cup sliced strawberries
Beverage		Beverage
Day 2		
½ cup juice-packed	Low-Salt Pizza (see page	2 ounces Grilled Pork
pineapple chunks	79)	Skewers (see page 85)
2 slices French Toast (see	12 grapes or cherries	1 cup buttered noodles
page 48)	1 piece chocolate snack	½ cup green beans
1 tablespoon margarine	cake	½ cup cucumber and
or butter	Beverage	onions
Low-sugar syrup		½ cup ice cream
Beverage		Beverage
Day 3		
½ grapefruit	2 ounces sliced turkey	Spaghetti with tomato sauce
1 poached egg	1 hard roll	2 ounces meatballs
1 English muffin, toasted	1 teaspoon mayonnaise	½ cup zucchini
1 tablespoon margarine	Lettuce	1 cup mixed salad greens
or butter	1 apple	2 tablespoons salad dressing
Low-sugar jelly	2 sugar cookies	1 slice garlic French bread
Beverage	Beverage	½ cup juice-packed canned
		peaches
		Beverage

Sample 80-Gram Protein Diet

Breakfast	Lunch	Dinner
Day 1		
½ cup apple juice	3-ounce ground beef patty	4 ounces Lemon-Garlic
1 egg, scrambled	1 hamburger bun	Cornish Hens (see page 101)
2 slices whole wheat bread, toasted	Mayonnaise, lettuce, onion	1 cup steamed rice
1 tablespoon margarine or butter	1 fresh pear	½ cup green peas
Low-sugar jelly	2 oatmeal cookies	½ cup cole slaw with carrots
Beverage	Beverage	1 slice pound cake
		½ cup sliced strawberries
		Beverage
Day 2		
½ cup juice-packed pineapple chunks	Low-Salt Pizza (see page 79)	4 ounces Grilled Pork Skewers (see page 85)
2 slices French Toast (see page 48)	12 grapes or cherries	1 cup buttered noodles
1 tablespoon margarine or butter	1 piece chocolate snack cake	½ cup green beans
Low-sugar syrup	Beverage	½ cup cucumber and onions
Beverage		1 sugar-free Popsicle
		Beverage
Day 3		
½ grapefruit	3 ounces sliced turkey	Spaghetti (garlic and olive oil on noodles)
1 poached egg	1 hard roll	4 ounces meatballs
1 English muffin, toasted	1 teaspoon mayonnaise	½ cup zucchini
1 tablespoon margarine or butter	Lettuce	1 cup mixed salad greens
Low-sugar jelly	1 apple	2 tablespoons low-sodium salad dressing
Beverage	2 sugar cookies	1 slice garlic French bread (no salt)
	Beverage	½ cup juice-packed canned peaches
		Beverage

Diabetes and Celiac Disease

In the 1950s, medical doctors in the United States began to recognize a disease called "gluten enteropathy," or nontropical sprue. It later became known as celiac sprue or celiac disease. Sometime in the 1980s, physicians were becoming aware that gluten enteropathy may have an influence in diabetes management. For many individuals with diabetes and for the health care team assisting in their management, following both a gluten-free diet and a diabetic diet may seem like an impossible task.

Although living with both diabetes and celiac disease can be challenging, it is not impossible. Celiac disease requires the avoidance of gluten protein found in wheat, oats, barley, and rye. The gluten damages the nutrient-absorbing lining of the small intestine, called microvilli. This damage leads to diarrhea, weight loss, and vitamin deficiencies. The vitamins most commonly deficient are B vitamins, especially folic acid. Poor digestive absorption causes abdominal distention, bloating, muscle wasting, and fatigue.

After a person with celiac disease starts a gluten-free diet, the small intestinal villi begin to return to normal. Usually, over a one- to three-month period, the person's health significantly improves. Consumption of hidden gluten will trigger symptoms in a short period of time, indicating the need to continue avoiding irritant foods.

Corn and rice are the usual starch substitutes for wheat, oats, barley, and rye. Many convenience products are made from these sources—pasta, breads, waffles. Some people may be misled into consuming millet and buckwheat as starches. While these grains may not contain irritating gluten proteins, they are processed in the same grinding devices as wheat and should be omitted from the diet because of the risk of cross-contamination (unless a mill designates that its grinding is for *only* nongluten grains).

People with diabetes and celiac disease can achieve a healthful diet with the help of mail-order supplies and a reliable food allergy cookbook like *Living with Food Allergies* (Contemporary Books, 1999). Many health food stores feature gluten-free items that, although they may not taste exactly the same as wheat items, are a more healthful alternative when gluten enteropathy complicates blood glucose management.

The argument continues as to how much gluten is too much. Since medical science still hasn't explained why some people do not tolerate wheat and others need to avoid gluten, much research is needed to answer these questions. Diets containing as little as 2 to 5 grams of gluten per day (one slice of bread may contain 1 gram of gluten) have been reported to cause gastrointestinal problems. In one case, an eight-year-old boy whose only apparent exposure to gluten was a once-weekly Holy Communion wafer exhibited poor growth and villi atrophy.

Suggested Gluten-Free Menus

Day 1	Day 2	Day 3
Breakfast: Grits, scrambled egg, orange juice	Breakfast: Yogurt, rice flour muffin, banana	Breakfast: Turkey sausage, rice bread, apple
Lunch: Taco salad with corn chips	Lunch: Tuna salad, potato chips, carrot salad	Lunch: Chef's salad, rice crackers
Dinner: Rib eye steak, corn, spinach, tomato salad	Dinner: Broiled salmon, baked potato, mixed vegetables	Dinner: Baked chicken, rice, broccoli, cucumber salad
Snack: Popcorn	Snack: Rice pudding	Snack: Rice flour cookie

Chapter 2
Menus

Week 1, Day 1

Breakfast
Berry-Banana Smoothie (see page 44)

Low-fat string mozzarella cheese

Beverage

Lunch
Veggie Roll-Ups (see page 124)

Apple

Beverage

Dinner
Rosemary Chicken (see page 91)

Deli-prepared sweet-potato salad

Steamed green beans

Coconut Cream Pudding (see page 159)

Beverage

Week 1, Day 2

Breakfast

Scrambled egg

Zucchini Bread (see page 64)

½ grapefruit

Beverage

Lunch

South of the Border Chicken Salad (see page 53)

Pear

Beverage

Dinner

Halibut Steaks and Pineapple Salsa (see page 102)

Avocado and Potato Salad (see page 60)

Carrot sticks, celery, and radishes

Chewy Nugget Bars (see page 152)

Beverage

Week 1, Day 3

Breakfast

Chocolate Pudding Cereal (see page 50)

Banana

Beverage

Lunch

Fresh-Vegetable Lasagna (see page 113)

Grapes

Beverage

Dinner

Pine-Nut-Stuffed Lamb Chops (see page 80)

Baked potato

Roasted Asparagus with Rosemary (see page 127)

Peach slices

Beverage

Week 1, Day 4

Breakfast

Whole-grain ready-to-eat cereal

Low-fat milk

Strawberries

Beverage

Lunch

Penne and Prosciutto in Cream Sauce (see page 88)

Tossed vegetable salad

Low-fat salad dressing

Plum

Beverage

Dinner

Crispy Thyme Chicken (see page 90)

Herb-Roasted Potatoes (see page 134)

Peas and carrots

Grapefruit Baked with Chocolate (see page 161)

Beverage

Week 1, Day 5

Breakfast

Oatmeal

Soy milk

Blueberries

Beverage

Lunch

Tofu Curry Dip (see page 72)

Raw vegetables: carrot sticks, celery, cherry tomatoes, cucumber slices

Chocolate Brownies (see page 154)

Beverage

Dinner

Cajun Pork Chops (see page 83)

Quinoa with Apricots and Pecans (see page 116)

Broccoli

Strawberry Pizza Dessert (see page 139)

Beverage

Week 1, Day 6

Breakfast

Orange juice

Crisp bacon

English muffin with apple butter

Beverage

Lunch

Penne with Spinach and Goat Cheese (see page 112)

Red grapes

Beverage

Dinner

Seafood Stew (see page 106)

Tossed vegetable salad

Low-fat salad dressing

Apple and Cranberry Compote (see page 166)

Beverage

Week 1, Day 7

Breakfast

Pancakes

Low-sugar syrup

Pork sausage

Melon wedge

Beverage

Lunch

Red Lentil Hash (see page 119)

Cole slaw

Mixed fresh berries

Beverage

Dinner

Oven-Fried Chicken (see page 92)

Pineapple Rice (see page 117)

Deli beet salad

Lemon Yogurt Bars (see page 153)

Beverage

Week 2, Day 1

Breakfast

Poached egg on toast

Strawberries

Beverage

Lunch

Black Bean Soup (see page 122)

Tomato and cucumber salad

Pineapple Bread (see page 65)

Beverage

Dinner

Grilled Pork Skewers (see page 85)

Buttered noodles

Garlic Sautéed Spinach and Onions (see page 136)

Bananas Flambé with Frozen Yogurt (see page 164)

Beverage

Week 2, Day 2

Breakfast

Whole-grain ready-to-eat cereal

Almond milk

Banana

Beverage

Lunch

Veggie Roll-Ups (see page 124)

Apple

Beverage

Dinner

Savory Garlic Shrimp (see page 109)

Lentil Salad (see page 58)

Stir-Fried Collards (see page 133)

Double Chocolate Cupcakes (see page 151)

Beverage

Week 2, Day 3

Breakfast

Peach Smoothie (see page 45)

Bran muffin

Beverage

Lunch

Tuna salad submarine sandwich

Potato chips

Orange wedges

Beverage

Dinner

Chicken in Fragrant Spices (see page 93)

Warm Potato Salad (see page 59)

Green Bean Salad with Tomatoes (see page 63)

Cherry Cobbler (see page 167)

Beverage

Week 2, Day 4

Breakfast

Oatmeal

Low-fat milk

Blueberries

Beverage

Lunch

Zippy Dip (see page 73)

Crackers or muffin

Raw vegetables

Mushroom-Barley Stew (see page 120)

Beverage

Dinner

Cajun Stir-Fry (see page 108)

Rice

Root Beer Float Cake (see page 144)

Beverage

Week 2, Day 5

Breakfast

French Toast (see page 48)

Low-sugar syrup

Crisp bacon

Beverage

Lunch

Sweet Potatoes over Rice (see page 115)

Tossed vegetable salad

Low-fat salad dressing

Beverage

Dinner

Spice-Rubbed Pork Chops (see page 84)

Apple-Mango Chutney (see page 75)

Parsley boiled potatoes

Green beans

Fruit Surprise Dessert (see page 162)

Beverage

Week 2, Day 6

Breakfast

Applesauce–Bran Cereal Muffins (see page 66)

String mozzarella cheese

Orange juice

Beverage

Lunch

Hamburger on bun

Lettuce and tomato

Munch Mix (see page 70)

Beverage

Dinner

Polynesian Turkey Kabobs (see page 99)

Buttered noodles

Steamed broccoli

Berries Macedonia (Fruit Compote) (see page 163)

Beverage

Week 2, Day 7

Breakfast

Chocolate-Banana Yogurt Shake (see page 46)

Granola bar

Beverage

Lunch

Tuna salad on whole wheat toast

Pear

Beverage

Dinner

Sweet-and-Sour Chicken (see page 94)

Rice

Peas and carrots

Mocha Snack Cake (see page 145)

Beverage

Week 3, Day 1

Breakfast

Banana Split Muffin Sundae (see page 51)

Beverage

Lunch

Salmon burger

Whole-grain bun

Cole slaw

Beverage

Dinner

Mediterranean Lemon Chicken (see page 97)

Pasta with Pesto (see page 111)

Carrots

Kiwi and strawberries

Beverage

Week 3, Day 2

Breakfast

Whole-grain ready-to-eat cereal

Almond milk

Strawberries

Beverage

Lunch

Curried Lentil Stew (see page 121)

Cucumber salad

Plum

Beverage

Dinner

Spiced Turkey Roast (see page 100)

Salt-Baked Rosemary Potatoes (see page 135)

Peas

Peanut Butter Cupcakes (see page 150)

Beverage

Week 3, Day 3

Breakfast

Oatmeal with raisins

Low-fat milk

½ pink grapefruit

Beverage

Lunch

Shrimp Chowder (see page 107)

Savory Breadsticks (see page 68)

Mango slices

Beverage

Dinner

Broiled steak fillet

Asparagus and Pistachio Risotto (see page 128)

Sliced tomato salad

Chewy Chocolate Gingerbread Cookies (see page 155)

Beverage

Week 3, Day 4

Breakfast

Waffles

Low-sugar syrup

Fresh fruit cup

Beverage

Lunch

Turkey and Bing Cherry Salad (see page 54)

Toasted English muffin

Butter or margarine

Beverage

Dinner

Smothered Pork Chops (see page 86)

Baked Sweet Potatoes Stuffed with Cranberries,
Pear, and Pecans (see page 137)

Mixed vegetable salad

Low-fat salad dressing

Chocolate Raspberry Cheesecake (see page 140)

Beverage

Week 3, Day 5

Breakfast

Mexican Eggs (see page 123)

Melon wedge

Beverage

Lunch

Low-Salt Pizza (see page 79)

Grapes

Beverage

Dinner

Lamb Chops with Mango-Mint Relish (see page 81)

Baked potato

Green beans

Pumpkin-Maple Cake (see page 147)

Beverage

Week 3, Day 6

Breakfast

French Toast (see page 48)

Low-sugar syrup

Bacon

Orange juice

Beverage

Lunch

Lemonade Turkey Salad (see page 56)

Roll

Mixed berries

Beverage

Dinner

Mongolian Hot Pot (see page 77)

Noodles

Rice Pudding (see page 160)

Beverage

Week 3, Day 7

Breakfast

Whole-grain ready-to-eat cereal

Soy milk

Banana

Beverage

Lunch

Chili con Carne (see page 78)

Crackers

Apple wedges

Beverage

Dinner

Grilled Chicken Sesame (see page 96)

Rice

Hot German Cabbage (see page 132)

Blueberry Loaf Cake (see page 148)

Beverage

Week 4, Day 1

Breakfast

Breakfast Hot Dog (see page 49)

Orange juice

Beverage

Lunch

Poppy Seed Citrus Turkey Salad (see page 55)

Muffin

Beverage

Dinner

Lamb Chops with Mint Salsa (see page 82)

Boiled potatoes

Peas and carrots

Chocolate Brownies (see page 154)

Beverage

Week 4, Day 2

Breakfast

Oatmeal with dried apricots

Low-fat milk

Beverage

Lunch

Tuna Niçoise Fusilli (see page 105)

Melon wedge

Beverage

Dinner

Crispy Peanut-Coconut Chicken (see page 95)

Barley-Rice Pilaf (see page 114)

Orange and Spinach Salad (see page 61)

Tropical Macedonia (see page 165)

Beverage

Week 4, Day 3

Breakfast

Strawberry-Banana Frosty (see page 47)

Beverage

Lunch

Easy Veggie Pizza (see page 125)

Plum

Beverage

Dinner

Paella (see page 98)

7-Up Cake (see page 146)

Beverage

Week 4, Day 4

Breakfast

Whole-grain ready-to-eat cereal

Almond milk

Blueberries

Beverage

Lunch

Orange and Basil Black Beans (see page 118)

Corn bread

Mango Salsa (see page 74)

Beverage

Dinner

Lemon-Garlic Cornish Hens (see page 101)

Baked potato

Roasted Asparagus Parmesan (see page 129)

Peanut Butter Oatmeal Cookies (see page 157)

Beverage

Week 4, Day 5

Breakfast

Almond-Raspberry Smoothie (see page 43)

Beverage

Lunch

Boiled Edamame (see page 71)

Insalata Caprese (see page 62)

Roll

Beverage

Dinner

Snapper with Pine Nuts and Olives (see page 104)

Rice

Marinated Broccoli (see page 131)

Corn Salsa (see page 76)

Banana Cake (see page 149)

Beverage

Week 4, Day 6

Breakfast

Raspberry Muffins (see page 67)

Grapefruit juice

Beverage

Lunch

Basil Shrimp Skewers (see page 110)

Black Bean and Barley Kwanzaa Salad (see page 57)

Beverage

Dinner

Zesty Pork Stew (see page 87)

Noodles

Green beans

Apple Crisp (see page 168)

Beverage

Week 4, Day 7

Breakfast

Pancakes

Low-sugar syrup

Turkey sausage

Melon wedge

Beverage

Lunch

Warm Chicken Salad (see page 52)

Green Bean and Cherry Tomato Casserole (see page 130)

Sugar-Free Chocolate Chip Cookies (see page 156)

Beverage

Dinner

South of the Border Pizza (see page 126)

Fresh fruit cup

Beverage

Chapter 3
Recipes

Smoothies, Shakes, and Frosties

Drinking one of these smoothies, shakes, or frosties is an easy and delicious way to start the morning with good nutrition. These recipes also make healthful and refreshing snacks.

Almond-Raspberry Smoothie

1 cup almond milk
6 ounces frozen unsweetened raspberries
1 banana, cut into chunks

Combine all ingredients in blender. Cover and blend until smooth.
Pour into 2 glasses.

Makes 2 servings.

One serving = 2 carbohydrates + 1 fat
Calories per serving = 219
Protein 5 g
Carbohydrates 27 g
Fat 8 g
Sodium 11 mg
Cholesterol 0 mg

Berry–Banana Smoothie

½ cup fresh or frozen blueberries
¼ small banana
½ cup unsweetened apple juice
½ cup low-fat vanilla yogurt
½ cup crushed ice

Combine all ingredients in blender. Cover and blend until smooth.
Serve immediately.

Makes 1 serving.

One serving = ½ milk + 2 fruits
Calories per serving = 154
Protein 5 g
Carbohydrates 22 g
Fat 3 g
Sodium 201 mg
Cholesterol 87 mg

Peach Smoothie

1 fresh peach, peeled and pit removed, or 10 frozen peach slices
(Unpeeled nectarine may be substituted.)
½ cup low-fat milk
1 tablespoon frozen orange juice concentrate
Artificial sweetener (optional)
4 to 6 ice cubes

Combine peach, milk, orange juice concentrate, and artificial sweetener
(if desired) in blender or food processor. Cover and blend until smooth.
Gradually add ice cubes and blend until smooth.

Makes 1 serving.

One serving = 2 fruits + ½ milk
Calories per serving = 157
Protein 4 g
Carbohydrates 27 g
Fat 2 g
Sodium 61 mg
Cholesterol 16 mg

Chocolate–Banana Yogurt Shake

½ cup low-fat vanilla yogurt
½ cup skim milk
½ small banana, cut into chunks
1 teaspoon sugar-free instant chocolate pudding mix

Combine all ingredients in blender or food processor.
Cover and blend until smooth.

Makes 1 serving.

One serving = 1 milk + 1 fruit
Calories per serving = 171
Protein 10 g
Carbohydrates 24 g
Fat 4 g
Sodium 203 mg
Cholesterol 16 mg

Strawberry–Banana Frosty

½ **cup unsweetened frozen strawberries, slightly thawed**
½ **small ripe banana**
¼ **cup fresh orange juice**

Place all ingredients in blender. Cover and puree until smooth.
Serve immediately.

Makes 1 serving.

One serving = 2 fruits
Calories per serving = 122
Protein 1 g
Carbohydrates 24 g
Fat 2 g
Sodium 12 mg
Cholesterol 0 mg

Breakfast and Brunch Treats

Vary your breakfast routine with one of the following recipes. They also make the centerpiece of a satisfying brunch or supper.

French Toast

1 egg
¼ cup low-fat milk
½ teaspoon sugar
¼ teaspoon ground cinnamon
2 slices French bread, 1 inch thick
1 teaspoon margarine or butter

Beat egg, milk, sugar, and cinnamon in bowl. Soak bread in mixture until saturated. Melt margarine in skillet. Cook bread slices over medium heat until golden brown on each side, about 10 minutes.
Serve hot with fruit, low-sugar syrup, or powdered sugar.

Makes 1 serving.

One serving = 1 medium-fat meat + 2 starch + 1 fat
Calories per serving = 297
Protein 10 g
Carbohydrates 35 g
Fat 6 g
Sodium 172 mg
Cholesterol 91 mg

Breakfast Hot Dog

2 turkey sausage breakfast links
1 hot dog roll
1 tablespoon shredded low-fat cheddar cheese

Cook sausage according to package directions. Heat or toast hot dog roll. Put sausage links in roll. Top with cheese. Toast to melt cheese, if desired.

Makes 1 serving.

One serving = 1 starch + 1 medium-fat meat + 1 fat
Calories per serving = 252
Protein 13 g
Carbohydrates 21 g
Fat 9 g
Sodium 580 mg
Cholesterol 21 mg

Chocolate Pudding Cereal

1 cup low-fat milk
3 tablespoons Cream of Wheat or Cream of Rice cereal
2 teaspoons no-calorie sweetener, such as Splenda
1 teaspoon unsweetened cocoa powder

Bring milk to boil in saucepan. Add cereal, sweetener, and cocoa powder.
Reduce heat to low. Simmer, stirring, until cereal thickens,
about 2 to 3 minutes.

Makes 1 serving.

One serving = 2 carbohydrates (or 1 starch + 1 low-fat milk)
Calories per serving = 231
Protein 9 g
Carbohydrates 34 g
Fat 4 g
Sodium 217 mg
Cholesterol 5 mg

Banana Split Muffin Sundae

1 banana-nut muffin
½ ripe banana
¼ cup low-fat vanilla yogurt
4 fresh strawberries
1 tablespoon fat-free whipped topping (optional)

Split muffin in half vertically, and place in banana split dish or oval bowl. Slice bananas around muffin halves. Top with yogurt. Slice strawberries over yogurt. Spoon on whipped topping, if desired.

Makes 1 serving.

One serving = 2 carbohydrates (or 1 starch + 1 fruit) + 1 fat
Calories per serving = 209
Protein 4 g
Carbohydrates 29 g
Fat 7 g
Sodium 306 mg
Cholesterol 39 mg

Salads

The salad recipes in this section include hearty main courses as well as lighter dinner salads.

Warm Chicken Salad

4 chicken thighs and drumsticks or 1 full chicken breast
1 clove garlic
1 romaine lettuce heart
¼ cup low-fat honey-mustard salad dressing
¼ cup low-fat lemon yogurt
8 radishes, sliced thin

Place chicken and garlic in large saucepan with enough water to cover them. Cook over medium heat, about 20 minutes. When chicken is tender, transfer to plate. When cool enough to handle, remove bones and skin. Cut into bite-size pieces. Chop lettuce into 2-inch pieces, and arrange on plates. Top with chicken. Mix honey-mustard salad dressing and yogurt until blended. Pour over chicken pieces. Top salads with radish slices. Serve immediately.

Makes 4 servings.

One serving = 3 lean meats + 1 vegetable + 1 fat
Calories per serving = 210
Protein 20 g
Carbohydrates 3 g
Fat 7 g
Sodium 167 mg
Cholesterol 98 mg

South of the Border Chicken Salad

½ cup tomato sauce
1 mild chili pepper, stemmed and seeded
1 clove garlic, minced
3 chicken breast halves
1 cup cubed Monterey Jack cheese (4 ounces)
½ yellow bell pepper, chopped
2 plum tomatoes, chopped
½ cup low-fat salad dressing

Combine tomato sauce, chili pepper, and garlic in skillet. Add chicken breasts, and poach over medium heat about 20 minutes. Remove chicken when fork-tender. Cool. Cube chicken and combine with cheese, yellow pepper, tomatoes, and salad dressing. Serve on lettuce.

Makes 3 servings.

One serving = 4 medium-fat meats + 1 fat
Calories per serving = 261
Protein 26 g
Carbohydrates 3 g
Fat 17 g
Sodium 279 mg
Cholesterol 168 mg

Turkey and Bing Cherry Salad

1 medium head romaine lettuce, chopped
¼ cup crumbled feta cheese
1 11-ounce can mandarin oranges
1 cup cubed roasted turkey breast
½ cup balsamic vinaigrette salad dressing
½ cup fresh or frozen Bing cherries, halved and pitted

Toss lettuce, cheese, oranges, turkey, and salad dressing together in large salad bowl. Arrange salad on individual plates. Sprinkle with cherries.

Makes 4 servings.

One serving = 3 lean meats + 2 vegetables + 1 fruit + 2 fats
Calories per serving = 362
Protein 24 g
Carbohydrates 18 g
Fat 11 g
Sodium 147 mg
Cholesterol 105 mg

Poppy Seed Citrus Turkey Salad

1 pound roasted turkey
1 ripe mango, peeled and pitted
1 ripe avocado, peeled and pitted
1 11-ounce can mandarin oranges, drained
½ cup raspberry vinaigrette salad dressing
2 teaspoons poppy seeds
4 large lettuce leaves

Cut turkey, mango, and avocado into bite-size cubes. Place in bowl with oranges, salad dressing, and poppy seeds. Toss gently.
Serve on lettuce leaves.

Makes 4 servings.

One serving = 4 lean meats + 1 fruit + 1 fat
Calories per serving = 313
Protein 27 g
Carbohydrates 12 g
Fat 16 g
Sodium 148 mg
Cholesterol 132 mg

Lemonade Turkey Salad

1 cup chopped cooked turkey
1 cup grapes, halved
¼ cup chopped celery
1 tablespoon vegetable oil
2 tablespoons frozen lemonade concentrate, thawed

Combine all ingredients in mixing bowl. Toss gently to mix.
Chill until ready to serve.

Makes 2 servings.

One serving = 3 lean meats + 1 fruit + 1 fat
Calories per serving = 253
Protein 22 g
Carbohydrates 13 g
Fat 13 g
Sodium 77 mg
Cholesterol 87 mg

Black Bean and Barley Kwanzaa Salad

½ cup quick-cooking barley
1 cup water
1 cup canned black beans, drained and rinsed
1 large green bell pepper, chopped
2 tablespoons chopped fresh parsley
1 shallot or green onion, finely chopped
¼ cup low-fat vinaigrette salad dressing
Hot pepper sauce, to taste

Pour barley into boiling water in saucepan. Simmer 8 to 10 minutes, until tender. Meanwhile, combine beans, green pepper, parsley, shallot or green onion, salad dressing, and hot pepper sauce in mixing bowl.
Drain barley, and add to vegetable mixture.
Toss to combine; may be served either warm or chilled.

Makes 4 servings.

One serving = 1 starch + 1 fat
Calories per serving = 86
Protein 2 g
Carbohydrates 12 g
Fat 4 g
Sodium 79 mg
Cholesterol 0 mg

Lentil Salad

½ cup brown or green lentils

2 cups water

1 bay leaf

1 teaspoon fresh thyme leaves or ¼ teaspoon dried thyme

2 plum tomatoes, chopped

½ cup chopped celery

½ cup chopped green or yellow bell pepper

3 tablespoons low-fat vinaigrette salad dressing

½ teaspoon Dijon mustard

Combine lentils in saucepan with water, bay leaf, and thyme.
Cook over medium heat 12 to 15 minutes, or until tender. Stir occasionally.
While lentils cook, combine tomatoes, celery, pepper, salad dressing, and
mustard in mixing bowl. Drain lentils. Discard bay leaf.
Add lentils to ingredients in bowl. Toss gently. Serve hot or cold.

Makes 2 servings.

One serving = 1 starch + 1 vegetable + 1 fat

Calories per serving = 190

Protein 14 g

Carbohydrates 24 g

Fat 8 g

Sodium 58 mg

Cholesterol 0 mg

Warm Potato Salad

1½ pounds potatoes, chopped
2 tablespoons olive oil
2 scallions, trimmed and thinly sliced
½ teaspoon salt
¼ teaspoon paprika

Bring a saucepan of water to a boil and add potatoes. Boil potatoes until fork-tender. Drain in colander. Let rest until cool enough to handle, about 15 to 20 minutes. Peel off skins, and slice ½ inch thick. Arrange potatoes on plate. Drizzle with olive oil; sprinkle with scallions, salt, and paprika. Serve immediately.

Makes 4 servings.

One serving = 1 starch + 1 fat
Calories per serving = 148
Protein 2 g
Carbohydrates 18 g
Fat 8 g
Sodium 197 mg
Cholesterol 0 mg

Avocado and Potato Salad

3 medium red potatoes, unpeeled
1 avocado, peeled, pitted, and cubed
¼ cup chopped onion
¼ cup chopped fresh cilantro or parsley leaves
½ cup honey-mustard salad dressing

Cut potatoes into 1-inch cubes. Cover with water, and cook over medium heat until tender. Pour off water. Cool. Combine potatoes, avocado, onion, cilantro or parsley, and salad dressing in mixing bowl.
Toss gently. Serve immediately.

Makes 4 servings.

One serving = 1 starch + 3 fats
Calories per serving = 205
Protein 4 g
Carbohydrates 27 g
Fat 11 g
Sodium 287 mg
Cholesterol 0 mg

Orange and Spinach Salad

4 cups fresh spinach leaves
1 small red onion, thinly sliced
½ cup white mushrooms, thinly sliced
2 navel oranges, peeled and thinly sliced
¼ cup chopped pecans, toasted
½ cup low-fat raspberry vinaigrette salad dressing

Place spinach leaves in large salad bowl. Top with onions, mushrooms, orange slices, and pecans. Pour salad dressing over salad. Serve immediately.

Makes 4 servings

One serving = 1 vegetable + 1 fat
Calories per serving = 67
Protein 2 g
Carbohydrates 8 g
Fat 7 g
Sodium 231 mg
Cholesterol 0 mg

Insalata Caprese

2 medium-size ripe tomatoes
4 ounces fresh mozzarella cheese
8 fresh basil leaves
¼ cup low-fat Italian salad dressing

Cut each tomato into 4 slices. Cut cheese into 8 slices. Layer tomato slice, cheese slice, and basil leaf four times. Serve with salad dressing.

Makes 2 servings.

One serving = 2 medium-fat meats + 1 vegetable + 1 fat
Calories per serving = 241
Protein 16 g
Carbohydrates 7 g
Fat 17 g
Sodium 497 mg
Cholesterol 69 mg

Green Bean Salad with Tomatoes

½ **pound green beans**
1 **medium tomato, cut into wedges**
¼ **cup low-fat vinaigrette salad dressing**

Steam green beans until tender. Cool. Place green beans and tomato wedges on salad plate. Pour salad dressing over vegetables.

Makes 3 servings.

One serving = 1 vegetable + 1 fat
Calories per serving = 66
Protein 1 g
Carbohydrates 4 g
Fat 4 g
Sodium 52 mg
Cholesterol 0 mg

Breads and Muffins

These tasty recipes make great breads and muffins to accompany your meals.

Zucchini Bread

2 eggs
⅓ cup vegetable oil
1¼ cups no-calorie sweetener, such as Splenda
1 cup unsweetened applesauce
2 cups unpeeled shredded zucchini
2 cups all-purpose flour
½ teaspoon baking powder
1 teaspoon baking soda
1 teaspoon ground cinnamon

Preheat oven to 375°F. Beat together eggs, oil, sweetener, applesauce, and zucchini. Add flour, baking powder, baking soda, and cinnamon. Mix well. Pour into lightly oiled 9″ × 5″ loaf pan. Bake 50 to 60 minutes, or until toothpick inserted into center comes out clean. Let cool 5 minutes in pan on wire rack. Remove from pan. Cool completely before slicing.

Makes 12 servings.

One serving = 1 starch + 1 fruit + 1 fat
Calories per serving = 179
Protein 3 g
Carbohydrates 28 g
Fat 6 g
Sodium 64 mg
Cholesterol 51 mg

Pineapple Bread

⅓ cup sugar
⅓ cup vegetable oil
2 eggs
2 cups all-purpose flour
1 tablespoon baking powder
1 cup crushed pineapple in juice, undrained

Preheat oven to 350°F. Beat together sugar, vegetable oil, and eggs. Add flour, baking powder, and pineapple with juice. Mix well. Pour into oiled 9″ × 5″ loaf pan. Bake 50 to 55 minutes, or until toothpick inserted into center comes out clean. Cool in pan 5 minutes on wire rack. Remove from pan. Cool completely before slicing.

Makes 12 servings.

One serving = 1 starch + 1 fruit + 1 fat
Calories per serving = 98
Protein 2 g
Carbohydrates 16 g
Fat 4 g
Sodium 103 mg
Cholesterol 0 mg

Applesauce–Bran Cereal Muffins

¾ cup all-purpose flour

2 teaspoons baking powder

1 cup raisin bran cereal

½ cup low-fat milk

¼ cup unsweetened applesauce

1 egg

2 tablespoons vegetable oil

Preheat oven to 400°F. Line muffin pan with paper muffin cups. Combine flour, baking powder, and cereal in mixing bowl. Add milk, and let stand 3 minutes. Stir in applesauce, egg, and vegetable oil. Batter will be lumpy. Spoon batter into lined muffin pan, filling each cup two-thirds full. Bake 15 to 20 minutes, or until golden brown.

Makes 6 muffins.

One muffin = 1 starch + 1 fat

Calories per muffin = 132

Protein 2 g

Carbohydrates 18 g

Fat 8 g

Sodium 149 mg

Cholesterol 22 mg

Raspberry Muffins

1 cup all-purpose flour
1½ teaspoons baking powder
½ teaspoon ground nutmeg
¼ cup vegetable oil
⅓ cup sugar
1 egg
½ cup apple juice
1 cup fresh or frozen raspberries (thawed)

Preheat oven to 375°F. Line muffin pan with paper muffin cups. Mix flour, baking powder, and nutmeg in mixing bowl. Add oil, sugar, egg, and apple juice. Stir until blended. Gently fold in raspberries. Spoon into muffin cups. Bake about 15 minutes, or until browned.

Makes 12 muffins.

One muffin = 1 starch + 1 fruit + 1 fat
Calories per serving = 178
Protein 3 g
Carbohydrates 28 g
Fat 8 g
Sodium 49 mg
Cholesterol 11 mg

Savory Breadsticks

1 pound frozen bread dough, thawed

2 teaspoons sesame seeds

1 teaspoon poppy seeds

2 teaspoons dried Italian herbs (or 1 teaspoon dried basil plus
1 teaspoon dried oregano)

1 egg white, slightly beaten

Cut dough into 24 pieces. On floured surface, roll each piece into 12-inch stick. Place 1 inch apart on lightly oiled baking sheet. In small bowl, mix sesame seeds, poppy seeds, and herbs. Brush breadsticks with egg white, and sprinkle with herb mixture. Allow breadsticks to rise 15 to 20 minutes in warm place. Meanwhile, preheat oven to 350°F.
Bake 12 to 15 minutes, or until golden brown.

Makes 24 servings.

One serving = 1 starch
Calories per serving = 78
Protein 2 g
Carbohydrates 19 g
Fat 2 g
Sodium 137 mg
Cholesterol 0 mg

Snacks and Relishes

With these sweet and savory ideas, snacking can be both nutritious and fun! Experiment with the relishes to give your meals exciting flavor yet little fat or sodium.

Parmesan Pita Snacks

3 6½-inch whole wheat pita bread rounds
¼ cup grated Parmesan cheese
1 tablespoon fresh oregano leaves or 1½ teaspoons dried oregano

Preheat oven to 400°F. Cut each pita bread round into 6 wedges. Place wedges onto baking sheet. Sprinkle with cheese and oregano. Bake about 5 minutes or until pita wedges are browned and crisp.

Makes 6 servings (3 wedges each).

One serving = 1 starch
Calories per serving = 96
Protein 4 g
Carbohydrates 17 g
Fat 2 g
Sodium 147 mg
Cholesterol 4 mg

Munch Mix

2 cups spoon-size shredded wheat cereal
½ cup small unsalted pretzels
1 cup air-popped popcorn
2 tablespoons nut or herb oil (such as walnut, thyme, or rosemary)
2 teaspoons Worcestershire sauce

Preheat oven to 350°F. Mix cereal, pretzels, and popcorn in 13″ × 9″ baking pan. Drizzle with oil and Worcestershire sauce. Toss to coat. Bake 15 minutes or until crisp. Cool. Store in covered container.

Makes 6 servings.

One serving = 1 starch + 1 fat
Calories per serving = 105
Protein 2 g
Carbohydrates 18 g
Fat 6 g
Sodium 154 mg
Cholesterol 0 mg

Boiled Edamame

4 cups water
1 tablespoon kosher salt
3 cups fresh green soybeans, in the pod

Bring water and salt to boil in large saucepan. Add soybeans. Bring water back to boil, and cook 4 minutes. Turn off heat, and let undrained soybeans cool. Place beans in storage container, along with enough cooking liquid to cover completely. Refrigerate until ready to eat. Edamame is best consumed the day it is made. Discard any leftovers not eaten by the fourth day.

Makes 4 servings.

One serving = ½ starch
Calories per serving = 31
Protein 3 g
Carbohydrates 6 g
Fat 1 g
Sodium 64 mg
Cholesterol 0 mg

Tofu Curry Dip

1 12.3-ounce package firm tofu
2 tablespoons chopped green onion
3 tablespoons currants or raisins
¼ cup unsweetened shredded coconut
1½ teaspoons mild curry powder
Raw vegetables: carrot sticks, celery sticks, cucumber slices, and
cherry tomatoes

Combine tofu, green onion, currants or raisins, coconut, and curry powder in
food processor. Blend until well mixed and creamy. Serve with vegetables.

Makes about 1½ cups (6 ¼-cup servings).

One serving = 1 lean meat + 1 carbohydrate (or 1 starch)
Calories per serving = 74
Protein 4 g
Carbohydrates 14 g
Fat 4 g
Sodium 164 mg
Cholesterol 0 mg

Zippy Dip

8 ounces low-fat cream cheese
2 tablespoons finely chopped green onion
1 to 2 teaspoons prepared mustard
1 teaspoon horseradish (optional)
½ teaspoon garlic powder
1 to 2 teaspoons low-fat milk, if needed

In a blender, blend together thoroughly cream cheese, green onion, mustard, horseradish (if desired), and garlic powder. Add 1 to 2 teaspoons low-fat milk, if needed, to blend smooth. Serve with raw vegetables and/or crackers.

Makes about 1 cup (4 ¼-cup servings).

One serving = 1 fat
Calories per serving = 64
Protein 1 g
Carbohydrates 1 g
Fat 6 g
Sodium 74 mg
Cholesterol 2 mg

Mango Salsa

1 ripe mango, peeled, pitted, and diced (almost 1½ cups)
2 tablespoons finely chopped onion
1 medium clove garlic, minced
2 tablespoons minced fresh cilantro

Combine all ingredients in mixing bowl.
Cover and refrigerate until ready to serve.

Makes 6 servings (¼ cup, as relish with meat dishes).

One serving = 1 fruit
Calories per serving = 76
Protein 1 g
Carbohydrates 14 g
Fat 0 g
Sodium 3 mg
Cholesterol 0 mg

Apple-Mango Chutney

1 tablespoon vegetable oil
2 tablespoons finely chopped onion
1 tablespoon grated fresh gingerroot
1 apple, peeled, cored, and diced
1 ripe mango, peeled, pitted, and diced
¼ cup apple juice
1 tablespoon finely chopped fresh cilantro

Place oil in saucepan over high heat. Add onion and ginger. Sauté until softened, 2 to 3 minutes. Stir in apple, mango, and apple juice. Sauté 3 minutes till fruit is soft. Pour into bowl. Cool. Fold in cilantro. Serve with Spice-Rubbed Pork Chops (see Index).

Makes about 4 servings (½ cup, as relish with meat dishes).

One serving = 1 fruit
Calories per serving = 93
Protein 1 g
Carbohydrates 21 g
Fat 2 g
Sodium 141 mg
Cholesterol 0 mg

Corn Salsa

1 cup fresh or frozen corn kernels
1 small ripe papaya, seeded and diced
½ cup finely chopped onion
2 plum tomatoes, seeded and diced
1 small clove garlic, minced
½ cup chopped fresh cilantro leaves

Cook corn until tender. Cool. Add papaya, onion, tomatoes, garlic, and cilantro. Cover and refrigerate at least 1 hour before serving.

Makes 6 servings (½ cup each).

One serving = 1 starch + 1 fruit
Calories per serving = 131
Protein 2 g
Carbohydrates 23 g
Fat 1 g
Sodium 47 mg
Cholesterol 0 mg

Meats, Poultry, and Fish

Use these recipes to create a wide variety of delicious main courses.
In addition to tasting great, they're easy to make.

Mongolian Hot Pot

4 cups low-sodium chicken broth
2 thin slices fresh gingerroot
1 clove garlic, minced
3 cups bite-size napa (Chinese) cabbage pieces
3 cups fresh spinach, stems removed
1 pound raw beef flank steak, cut into paper-thin slices
Chinese hot sauce, to taste
Low-sodium soy sauce (optional)

Combine chicken broth, gingerroot, and garlic in large saucepan. Bring to
boil over high heat. Add napa cabbage, spinach, sliced beef, and hot sauce.
Continue to cook over medium heat until meat is tender. Serve from
saucepan with ladle or slotted spoon. Pass soy sauce for dipping, if desired.
Serve with rice or noodles.

Makes 4 servings.

One serving = 3 medium-fat meats + 1 vegetable
Calories per serving = 261
Protein 20 g
Carbohydrates 4 g
Fat 18 g
Sodium 241 mg
Cholesterol 74 mg

Chili con Carne

1 pound lean ground beef
1 large onion, chopped
1 6-ounce can tomato paste
1½ to 2 tablespoons chili powder
½ teaspoon garlic powder
¼ teaspoon ground cumin
4 cups water

Brown ground beef in large saucepan.
Add onion, tomato paste, chili powder, garlic powder, cumin, and water.
Simmer over medium heat 3 to 4 minutes till onions are tender.

Makes 4 servings.

One serving = 3 medium-fat meats + 1 vegetable
Calories per serving = 271
Protein 24 g
Carbohydrates 2 g
Fat 20 g
Sodium 76 mg
Cholesterol 68 mg

Low-Salt Pizza

1 frozen pizza crust
½ 4-ounce can tomato paste
¼ cup water
¼ teaspoon dried oregano
2 teaspoons olive oil
½ pound lean ground beef, cooked and drained
4 ounces low-fat mozzarella cheese, shredded

Preheat oven to 400°F. Place pizza crust on large baking sheet. Combine tomato paste, water, oregano, and olive oil in small bowl. Mix well. Pour over crust, and spread evenly. Sprinkle with ground beef and then with cheese. Bake 20 to 30 minutes, or until crust is golden brown. Cut into 12 pieces.

Makes 4 servings.

One serving = 2 medium-fat meats + 1 starch + 1 fat
Calories per serving = 267
Protein 16 g
Carbohydrates 19 g
Fat 14 g
Sodium 212 mg
Cholesterol 97 mg

Pine-Nut-Stuffed Lamb Chops

4 lamb chops, cut 1 inch thick
1 tablespoon butter or margarine
1 teaspoon fresh oregano leaves or ¼ teaspoon dried oregano
¼ cup pine nuts
1 clove garlic, minced

With sharp knife, cut horizontal pocket in each lamb chop, starting at fat
edge and cutting to bone. Set chops aside. Melt butter in skillet.
Add oregano, pine nuts, and garlic. Cook over medium heat, stirring
frequently, until nuts are golden brown. Remove from heat. Spoon mixture
into lamb chop pockets. Place each chop on grill or broiling pan.
Grill or broil 4 inches away from heat about 5 minutes.
Turn and continue cooking 5 minutes longer until chops are well browned.

Makes 2 servings.

One serving = 4 medium-fat meats + 1 fat
Calories per serving = 319
Protein 26 g
Carbohydrates 1 g
Fat 7 g
Sodium 81 mg
Cholesterol 131 mg

Lamb Chops with Mango-Mint Relish

1 ripe mango, peeled, pitted, and diced
1 small garlic clove, minced
1 ounce pine nuts, toasted and chopped
10 fresh mint leaves, chopped
4 lamb chops

Combine mango, garlic, pine nuts, and mint leaves in small bowl. To allow
flavors to blend before serving, let stand at room temperature
while broiling or grilling lamb chops.

Makes 2 servings.

One serving = 3 medium-fat meats + 1 fruit
Calories per serving = 294
Protein 24 g
Carbohydrates 12 g
Fat 18 g
Sodium 111 mg
Cholesterol 132 mg

Lamb Chops with Mint Salsa

½ cup chopped fresh mint leaves
¼ cup chopped fresh parsley
6 baby gherkins (cornichons)
1 teaspoon capers
3 tablespoons olive oil
6 lamb chops

Preheat oven to 425°F. Process mint, parsley, gherkins, capers, and olive oil in food processor or blender until smooth. Coat each lamb chop with spoonful of mint salsa. Place in a pan, and roast 25 to 30 minutes. Serve remaining salsa with chops.

Makes 2 servings.

One serving = 3 medium-fat meats + 1 fat
Calories per serving = 287
Protein 24 g
Carbohydrates 3 g
Fat 17 g
Sodium 374 mg
Cholesterol 87 mg

Cajun Pork Chops

4 ½-inch-thick pork chops (about 4 ounces each)
1 small onion, sliced
1½ teaspoons poultry seasoning (or ¼ teaspoon dried thyme leaves,
¼ teaspoon ground sage, and ¼ teaspoon garlic powder)
¼ teaspoon ground cumin
2 to 3 drops hot pepper sauce

Preheat oven to 325°F. Arrange pork chops in single layer in 8-inch square
baking pan. Top each chop with onion slice. Sprinkle with poultry seasoning,
cumin, and hot pepper sauce. Cover with aluminum foil.
Bake 30 to 35 minutes, or until chops are tender.
Spoon baking juices over chops just before serving.

Makes 4 servings.

One serving = 3 lean meats
Calories per serving = 171
Protein 24 g
Carbohydrates 2 g
Fat 9 g
Sodium 147 mg
Cholesterol 126 mg

Spice-Rubbed Pork Chops

1 tablespoon hot Hungarian paprika
½ teaspoon ground ginger
1 teaspoon ground cinnamon
¼ teaspoon ground cloves
4 4-ounce bone-in pork chops
1 tablespoon vegetable oil

Preheat oven to 400°F. In small bowl, combine paprika, ginger, cinnamon, and cloves. Rub one side of each chop with spice mixture. Place medium-size ovenproof skillet over high heat, and add oil. When oil smokes, place chops in skillet, rubbed side down, and sear meat 30 seconds. Turn chops over. Place pan in oven until interior temperature of meat reaches 160°F, about 10 minutes. Serve with Apple-Mango Chutney (see Index).

Makes 4 servings.

One serving = 3 lean meats
Calories per serving = 174
Protein 26 g
Carbohydrates 2 g
Fat 5 g
Sodium 81 mg
Cholesterol 98 mg

Grilled Pork Skewers

1 pound thick-cut pork chops
10 to 12 fresh bay leaves or basil leaves
1 tablespoon olive oil

Heat grill with rack about 4 inches from heat. Cut pork into 1-inch cubes. Skewer meat alternately with bay leaves or basil leaves. Baste with olive oil, and grill 4 to 5 minutes on each side. Remove from heat and serve.

Makes 2 servings.

One serving = 4 lean meats
Calories per serving = 227
Protein 29 g
Carbohydrates 0 g
Fat 16 g
Sodium 108 mg
Cholesterol 114 mg

Smothered Pork Chops

2 4-ounce pork chops
1 orange
½ teaspoon Italian seasoning
1 onion, sliced thin

In large skillet, brown pork chops over medium-high heat. Squeeze orange juice over pork chops. Sprinkle with Italian seasoning. Add onion. Cover and reduce heat to simmer. Cook 20 to 25 minutes, until chops are tender.

Makes 2 servings.

One serving = 3 medium-fat meats
Calories per serving = 203
Protein 18 g
Carbohydrates 2 g
Fat 11 g
Sodium 71 mg
Cholesterol 78 mg

Zesty Pork Stew

1 pound lean pork tenderloin, cut into 1-inch cubes
2 small sweet potatoes, peeled and cubed
1 small green bell pepper, chopped
1 cup coarsely chopped cabbage
1 teaspoon Cajun seasoning
1 cup water

Combine all ingredients in large saucepan. Cook over medium heat until sweet potatoes are tender, 15 to 20 minutes.

Makes 4 servings.

One serving = 3 lean meats + 1 starch + 1 vegetable
Calories per serving = 291
Protein 25 g
Carbohydrates 24 g
Fat 17 g
Sodium 417 mg
Cholesterol 79 mg

Penne and Prosciutto in Cream Sauce

12 ounces penne or other tubular pasta
¼ cup chopped fresh cilantro or green onion
½ pound prosciutto, cut into matchsticks
¼ cup grated Parmesan cheese
1 cup frozen asparagus cuts, thawed
1 cup prepared cream sauce

Preheat oven to 350°F. Cook pasta according to package directions. Drain.
Combine with cilantro or green onion, prosciutto, cheese, asparagus, and
sauce. Toss gently. Pour into lightly oiled casserole dish.
Bake 10 minutes, or until top is brown.

Makes 4 servings.

One serving = 3 starches + 3 medium-fat meats + 1 fat
Calories per serving = 493
Protein 27 g
Carbohydrates 36 g
Fat 19 g
Sodium 448 mg
Cholesterol 89 mg

Basil–Garlic Chicken

6 garlic cloves, sliced thin
3 tablespoons chopped fresh basil leaves
1 3- to 4-pound chicken, cut into pieces
¼ cup orange juice or water

Preheat oven to 350°F. Combine garlic and basil in bowl.
Place chicken pieces into cooking bag or onto parchment paper.
Sprinkle with garlic and basil mixture. Add orange juice for moisture.
Close cooking bag, or seal parchment paper. Bake 40 to 50 minutes.

Makes 5 servings.

One serving = 3 lean meats
Calories per serving = 158
Protein 24 g
Carbohydrates 1 g
Fat 7 g
Sodium 162 mg
Cholesterol 157 mg

Crispy Thyme Chicken

4 boneless, skinless chicken breast halves
½ cup low-sugar cereal, such as corn flakes or Grape-Nuts
1 teaspoon fresh thyme leaves or ½ teaspoon dried thyme
1 tablespoon olive oil

Preheat oven to 400°F. Rinse chicken in water. Set aside. Combine cereal, thyme, and olive oil in blender. Blend on low speed until cereal is finely crushed. Pour cereal mixture onto a plate or into a bowl. Dip chicken into cereal mixture, coating both sides. Place in lightly oiled baking pan. Bake 25 to 30 minutes, or until chicken is cooked thoroughly.

Makes 4 servings.

One serving = 3 lean meats + 1 starch + 1 fat
Calories per serving = 197
Protein 24 g
Carbohydrates 12 g
Fat 6 g
Sodium 205 mg
Cholesterol 66 mg

Rosemary Chicken

1 3- to 4-pound chicken, cut into pieces
½ cup white wine or apple juice
2 tablespoons brown sugar
2 tablespoons vegetable oil
2 tablespoons fresh rosemary leaves or 2 teaspoons crushed
dried rosemary

Preheat oven to 350°F. Place chicken pieces in baking pan, skin side down. Combine wine or juice, sugar, vegetable oil, and rosemary in mixing bowl. Pour over chicken. Bake 15 minutes. Turn chicken pieces, and baste with available juices. Bake 20 minutes longer, or until done.

Makes 5 servings.

One serving = 3 lean meats
Calories per serving = 261
Protein 24 g
Carbohydrates 3 g
Fat 8 g
Sodium 111 mg
Cholesterol 127 mg

Oven-Fried Chicken

1 3-pound frying chicken, cut up
¼ cup olive oil
1 teaspoon dried thyme
½ teaspoon garlic powder

Preheat oven to 425°F. Rinse chicken pieces. Place olive oil in 13″ × 9″ baking pan. Turn chicken around in pan to coat with oil. Sprinkle chicken with thyme and garlic powder. Bake 30 minutes. Turn each piece of chicken, and continue baking 15 to 20 minutes longer, or until chicken is tender.

Makes 5 servings.

One serving = 3 lean meats
Calories per serving = 166
Protein 22 g
Carbohydrates 1 g
Fat 6 g
Sodium 108 mg
Cholesterol 119 mg

Chicken in Fragrant Spices

1 pound boneless, skinless chicken breasts
2 garlic cloves, sliced thin
1 teaspoon ground ginger
1 teaspoon ground cumin
¼ teaspoon ground turmeric
¼ cup low-fat plain or vanilla yogurt

Prepare grill or preheat oven to 350°F. Make three to four diagonal slashes in each chicken breast. Stuff slices of garlic into each slash. Combine ginger, cumin, and turmeric in small bowl. Rub mixture onto surface of each chicken breast. Grill or bake 4 to 5 minutes, turn each piece, and continue cooking 4 to 5 minutes, or until chicken is tender. Just before serving, top each chicken breast with 1 tablespoon yogurt.

Makes 4 servings.

One serving = 3 lean meats
Calories per serving = 148
Protein 24 g
Carbohydrates 1 g
Fat 9 g
Sodium 62 mg
Cholesterol 92 mg

Sweet-and-Sour Chicken

1 pound boneless, skinless chicken breasts
1 20-ounce can juice-packed pineapple chunks
¼ cup sugar
2 tablespoons cornstarch
½ cup vinegar
1 green bell pepper, sliced
1 medium onion, sliced thin

Cut chicken into ½-inch cubes. Combine pineapple chunks with their juice,
sugar, cornstarch, and vinegar in large skillet. Add chicken.
Cook over medium heat 5 to 7 minutes, stirring frequently as sauce thickens.
Add green pepper and onion. Cook 5 minutes longer, or
until vegetables and chicken are tender.

Makes 4 servings.

One serving = 3 lean meats + 1 fruit
Calories per serving = 211
Protein 26 g
Carbohydrates 13 g
Fat 11 g
Sodium 98 mg
Cholesterol 116 mg

Crispy Peanut-Coconut Chicken

¼ cup flaked coconut
½ cup salted peanuts
1 teaspoon grated fresh gingerroot or ¼ teaspoon ground ginger
1 egg
1 pound boneless, skinless chicken breast, cut into 1-inch strips

Preheat oven to 400°F. Finely chop coconut, peanuts, and ginger in food processor or blender. Pour onto waxed paper. Beat egg in bowl. Dip chicken pieces in egg, and then press into peanut mixture. Arrange on lightly oiled baking sheet. Bake 15 to 20 minutes, until chicken is tender and browned.

Makes 4 servings.

One serving = 3 lean meats + 1 fat
Calories per serving = 227
Protein 25 g
Carbohydrates 3 g
Fat 12 g
Sodium 298 mg
Cholesterol 87 mg

Grilled Chicken Sesame

2 4-ounce boneless, skinless chicken breast halves
1 teaspoon orange-flavored olive oil or pure olive oil (see Note)
2 teaspoons sesame seeds, toasted
⅛ teaspoon ground ginger
1 tablespoon honey

Prepare grill or broiler. Using a mallet or rolling pin, flatten chicken pieces to ¼ inch thick. Combine oil, sesame seeds, ginger, and honey in small bowl. Spoon onto chicken. Grill or broil 10 to 12 minutes on each side, or until tender. Just before serving, top with any remaining oil and honey mixture.

Makes 2 servings.

One serving = 3 lean meats
Calories per serving = 181
Protein 22 g
Carbohydrates 6 g
Fat 10 g
Sodium 67 mg
Cholesterol 71 mg

Note: Flavored olive oil is available from Eatzi's Market and Bakery (www.eatzis.com) and many local gourmet food shops.

Mediterranean Lemon Chicken

1 pound boneless, skinless chicken breasts
1 tablespoon lemon pepper oil (see Note)
1 fennel bulb, sliced thin
1 garlic clove, minced
2 teaspoons capers

Rinse chicken breasts. Heat oil in large skillet. Sauté chicken in oil over medium heat 3 to 4 minutes. Turn and sauté 5 additional minutes over low heat. Add fennel and garlic. Cook until chicken is tender and fennel is translucent. Just before serving, top with capers.

Makes 4 servings.

One serving = 3 lean meats
Calories per serving = 171
Protein 19 g
Carbohydrates 2 g
Fat 13 g
Sodium 203 mg
Cholesterol 93 mg

Note: Flavored olive oil is available from Eatzi's Market and Bakery (www.eatzis.com) and many local gourmet food shops.

Paella

½ pound boneless, skinless chicken breast, cut into bite-size pieces
1 cup water
1 teaspoon salt
½ cup uncooked basmati rice
½ pound peeled and cleaned medium shrimp
½ cup frozen green peas
2 green onions, sliced thin

In a large pot, boil chicken in water and salt over medium heat about 10 minutes, or until tender. Add rice. Continue to cook over medium heat, covered, until rice is tender, about 15 to 20 minutes. Stir occasionally to prevent sticking. Add extra water, if needed. When rice is tender, add shrimp, peas, and green onions, and simmer until shrimp are pink and fork-tender. Remove from heat. Serve immediately.

Makes 4 servings.

One serving = 3 lean meats + 1 starch
Calories per serving = 251
Protein 27 g
Carbohydrates 19 g
Fat 14 g
Sodium 594 mg
Cholesterol 106 mg

Polynesian Turkey Kabobs

1 pound boneless uncooked turkey breast
1 20-ounce can juice-packed pineapple chunks, drained
1 large red bell pepper, cut into chunks
1 large green bell pepper, cut into chunks
2 tablespoons low-sugar orange marmalade
½ teaspoon ground ginger

Cut turkey into bite-size chunks. Thread turkey chunks onto skewers
alternately with pineapple and peppers. Melt marmalade.
Stir in ginger. Brush about half of marinade over kabobs.
Broil 4 inches from heat, 12 to 15 minutes. Turn; baste with marinade.
Broil 5 to 10 minutes longer, until turkey is tender.

Makes 4 servings.

One serving = 3 lean meats + 1 fruit
Calories per serving = 205
Protein 24 g
Carbohydrates 12 g
Fat 10 g
Sodium 41 mg
Cholesterol 94 mg

Spiced Turkey Roast

1 pound boneless uncooked turkey breast
2 teaspoons olive oil
2 teaspoons ground cinnamon
1 teaspoon ground cloves
½ teaspoon ground allspice
1 teaspoon cracked peppercorns

Preheat oven to 350°F. Rub turkey breast with oil. Combine cinnamon, cloves, allspice, and peppercorns in small bowl. Rub spice mixture onto turkey. Place turkey in baking pan. Roast 1 hour or until juices are clear.

Makes 4 servings.

One serving = 3 lean meats
Calories per serving = 153
Protein 19 g
Carbohydrates 1 g
Fat 8 g
Sodium 68 mg
Cholesterol 77 mg

Lemon-Garlic Cornish Hens

2 Rock Cornish game hens
2 lemons, sliced thin
4 garlic cloves, peeled
1 onion, sliced thin
2 sprigs fresh rosemary or 1 teaspoon dried rosemary
¼ cup apple juice or white wine

Preheat oven to 375°F. Place whole Cornish hens on parchment paper big enough to wrap them tightly. Divide lemon slices, garlic, onion, and rosemary between the two hens, stuffing mixture into the cavity of each. Pour juice or wine over hens, and seal parchment, tucking end flaps under. Bake 40 to 50 minutes. Open parchment, and test for doneness. Return to oven 10 minutes longer to brown hen. Before serving, remove herbal stuffing.

Makes 4 servings.

One serving = 4 lean meats
Calories per serving = 179
Protein 27 g
Carbohydrates 2 g
Fat 12 g
Sodium 142 mg
Cholesterol 116 mg

Halibut Steaks and Pineapple Salsa

2 6-ounce halibut steaks
1 cup crushed fresh pineapple or pineapple canned in juice
1 medium garlic clove, minced
2 tablespoons minced fresh mint leaves or 2 teaspoons dried mint
¼ cup minced green or red onion

Place halibut steaks on oiled baking sheet. Combine pineapple, garlic, mint, and onion in bowl. Toss and let stand while fish cooks. Broil halibut steaks 3 inches from heat source until fish flakes easily with fork.
Serve pineapple salsa alongside the halibut.

Makes 2 servings.

One serving = 4 lean meats + 1 fruit
Calories per serving = 191
Protein 27 g
Carbohydrates 12 g
Fat 2 g
Sodium 186 mg
Cholesterol 202 mg

Grilled Salmon Supreme

2 4-ounce salmon fillets
1½ tablespoons honey-mustard salad dressing
¼ teaspoon Old Bay seasoning
½ teaspoon dried thyme
1 medium tomato, cut into 6 thin wedges
1 medium onion, sliced thin

Prepare grill. Place salmon fillets on heavy-duty aluminum foil, skin side down. Combine salad dressing, Old Bay seasoning, and thyme in bowl. Spoon about half of mixture onto salmon. Grill salmon about 5 minutes over medium-hot fire. Place tomato wedges and onion slices on each fillet. Grill another 5 minutes, basting with remaining salad dressing mixture, until fillets flake when pierced with fork. Serve immediately.

Makes 2 servings.

One serving = 3 lean meats + 1 fat
Calories per serving = 194
Protein 24 g
Carbohydrates 2 g
Fat 10 g
Sodium 297 mg
Cholesterol 54 mg

Snapper with Pine Nuts and Olives

1 pound red snapper fillets
1 teaspoon black peppercorns
2 bay leaves
½ navel orange, unpeeled and sliced
2 tablespoons chopped ripe olives
2 tablespoons pine nuts

Preheat oven to 400°F. Place snapper fillets in middle of parchment paper large enough to wrap fish. Top with peppercorns, bay leaves, and orange slices. Seal parchment paper, and place on baking sheet with end folds tucked under. Bake 30 to 40 minutes. Open parchment paper. Carefully remove bay leaves and orange slices. Sprinkle with olives and pine nuts. Broil 3 minutes to brown nuts and top of fish. Serve immediately.

Makes 4 servings.

One serving = 3 lean meats
Calories per serving = 153
Protein 23 g
Carbohydrates 2 g
Fat 6 g
Sodium 157 mg
Cholesterol 93 mg

Tuna Niçoise Fusilli

½ cup diced fennel
½ cup diced green bell pepper
1 6-ounce can solid white meat tuna packed in water, drained and flaked
¼ cup pitted black olives, cut in half
2 tablespoons olive oil
1 tablespoon capers
6 ounces uncooked fusilli

Combine fennel, pepper, tuna, olives, olive oil, and capers in bowl. Bring saucepan of salted water to boil, and cook fusilli until tender. Drain. Add tuna and vegetables. Gently fold together with rubber scraper. Serve immediately.

Makes 3 servings.

One serving = 1 starch + 2 lean meats + 2 fats
Calories per serving = 279
Protein 16 g
Carbohydrates 18 g
Fat 16 g
Sodium 405 mg
Cholesterol 58 mg

Seafood Stew

¼ cup white wine or chicken broth
1 cup finely chopped green and red bell pepper
2 cups diced onion
1 cup chopped celery
1 clove garlic, minced
½ teaspoon Old Bay seasoning
2 cups canned tomatoes
1 pound fresh halibut or haddock or amberjack, cubed
1 pound peeled and deveined shrimp

Combine wine or broth, red and green pepper, onion, celery, garlic, Old Bay
seasoning, and tomatoes in large saucepan. Bring mixture to a boil.
Simmer 10 to 15 minutes, until vegetables are soft. Add fish and shrimp.
Lower heat to simmer, and cook 10 to 15 minutes longer
until shrimp are pink and tender.

Makes 6 servings.

One serving = 4 very lean meats
Calories per serving = 194
Protein 27 g
Carbohydrates 10 g
Fat 2 g
Sodium 297 mg
Cholesterol 99 mg

Shrimp Chowder

½ cup chopped celery
¼ cup finely chopped onion
1 tablespoon vegetable oil
8 ounces low-fat cream cheese
1 cup low-fat milk
1 large potato, peeled and cubed
¾ pound frozen cooked shrimp, thawed

In large saucepan, sauté celery and onion in oil. Add cream cheese and milk. Stir over low heat until cheese is melted. Add potato. Cook until potato cubes are tender, about 8 to 10 minutes over low heat. Stir in shrimp. Heat thoroughly and serve.

Makes 4 servings.

One serving = 3 lean meats + 1 starch + 2 fats
Calories per serving = 325
Protein 24 g
Carbohydrates 17 g
Fat 21 g
Sodium 197 mg
Cholesterol 127 mg

Cajun Stir-Fry

1 tablespoon vegetable oil
1 pound shrimp, shelled and deveined
1 14-ounce bag frozen broccoli florets
½ cup chopped onion
1 tablespoon Cajun seasoning

Preheat wok. Add oil and shrimp. Stir-fry until shrimp are pink.
Stir in broccoli, onion, and Cajun seasoning. Stir-fry 3 to 5 minutes
until vegetables are tender. Serve over rice.

Makes 3 servings.

One serving = 4 very lean meats + 2 vegetables + 1 fat
Calories per serving = 219
Protein 27 g
Carbohydrates 12 g
Fat 7 g
Sodium 674 mg
Cholesterol 137 mg

Savory Garlic Shrimp

1 tablespoon lemon pepper oil (see Note)
1 pound fresh shrimp, peeled, or frozen shrimp, thawed
2 tablespoons chopped green onion
1 tablespoon chopped fresh parsley

Heat oil in skillet over medium heat. Add shrimp and onion.
Sauté, stirring constantly, until shrimp are pink and tender.
Just before serving, top with parsley.

Makes 3 servings.

One serving = 3 lean meats
Calories per serving = 157
Protein 19 g
Carbohydrates 1 g
Fat 6 g
Sodium 174 mg
Cholesterol 156 mg

Note: Flavored oil is available from Eatzi's Market and Bakery
(www.eatzis.com) and many local gourmet food shops.

Basil Shrimp Skewers

¼ cup low-fat honey-mustard salad dressing
1 tablespoon chopped fresh basil leaves or 1 teaspoon dried basil
1 pound fresh or frozen shrimp, peeled and deveined

Combine all ingredients in shallow glass dish. Toss to coat shrimp. Cover and refrigerate 1 hour. Preheat grill. Remove shrimp from marinade, and thread onto skewers. Arrange skewers on grill. Brush with marinade during grilling. Cook 4 to 5 minutes on each side.

Makes 3 servings.

One serving = 3 lean meats
Calories per serving = 157
Protein 19 g
Carbohydrates 2 g
Fat 8 g
Sodium 287 mg
Cholesterol 147 mg

Vegetables and Vegetarian Delights

Vegetables are more than just side dishes. They also can be the basis of satisfying main courses packed with vitamins and minerals. When possible, for mouthwatering flavor and maximum nutrition, choose recipes that feature seasonal and locally grown produce.

Pasta with Pesto

¼ cup olive oil
¼ cup grated Parmesan cheese
¼ cup chopped fresh parsley
¼ cup chopped fresh basil leaves or 2 tablespoons dried basil
1 clove garlic, minced
1 pound pasta, uncooked

Combine olive oil, cheese, parsley, basil, and garlic in blender or food processor. Process until smooth. Cook pasta in unsalted boiling water according to package directions until fork tender. Drain pasta.
Toss with pesto sauce. Serve hot.

Makes 4 servings.

One serving = 2 starches + 1 medium-fat meat + 2 fats
Calories per serving = 368
Protein 14 g
Carbohydrates 33 g
Fat 12 g
Sodium 66 mg
Cholesterol 47 mg

Penne with Spinach and Goat Cheese

12 ounces penne or other tubular pasta

1 tablespoon olive oil

1 clove garlic, minced

1 pound fresh spinach leaves, washed, stems removed

¼ cup (2 ounces) goat cheese

1 tablespoon finely chopped fresh rosemary leaves or 1 teaspoon dried rosemary, crushed

¼ cup toasted pine nuts or walnuts

Cook pasta in boiling water according to package directions. While pasta is cooking, combine oil and garlic in skillet. Sauté 1 minute. Add spinach to skillet. Stir to coat spinach leaves. Add goat cheese and rosemary to spinach mixture. Drain pasta, and stir into spinach and goat cheese.

Just before serving, sprinkle with nuts.

Makes 4 servings.

One serving = 3 starches + 2 fats + 1 vegetable

Calories per serving = 380

Protein 18 g

Carbohydrates 48 g

Fat 12 g

Sodium 153 mg

Cholesterol 10 mg

Fresh-Vegetable Lasagna

1 27-ounce jar pasta sauce
4½ ounces (8 sheets) oven-ready, no-boil lasagna noodles
8 ounces low-fat ricotta cheese
¼ cup grated Parmesan cheese
½ cup shredded low-fat mozzarella cheese
1 cup sliced fresh mushrooms
½ cup shredded fresh zucchini
2 cups whole-leaf fresh spinach, stems removed

Preheat oven to 375°F. Lightly oil 3-inch-deep lasagna baking dish. Spread about ½ cup pasta sauce in bottom of pan. Layer four uncooked lasagna sheets on sauce. Spread ½ cup pasta sauce over noodles, and then half the ricotta cheese, half the Parmesan cheese, and half the mozzarella cheese. Spread with half the mushrooms, zucchini, and spinach. Layer remaining four lasagna sheets, and repeat layers of remaining sauce, cheeses, and vegetables. Cover with foil or lid. Bake 40 to 50 minutes.
Uncover and bake 5 minutes longer to brown top. Remove from oven.
Let stand 10 to 15 minutes before cutting.

Makes 6 servings.

One serving = 2 starches + 2 medium-fat meats + 2 vegetables
Calories per serving = 351
Protein 27 g
Carbohydrates 44 g
Fat 11 g
Sodium 353 mg
Cholesterol 84 mg

Barley-Rice Pilaf

1 tablespoon butter or margarine
1 small onion, chopped
⅓ cup barley
⅓ cup white rice
2 cups water
1 carrot, peeled and chopped
1 stalk celery, chopped
Salt and pepper (to taste)

Melt butter in saucepan over medium heat. Add onion. Sauté until onion is tender. Add barley, rice, water, carrot, celery, salt, and pepper. Bring to a boil. Reduce heat to simmer. Cover and cook 15 minutes, or until liquid is absorbed and vegetables are soft.

Makes 4 servings.

One serving = 1 starch + 1 vegetable
Calories per serving = 141
Protein 3 g
Carbohydrates 25 g
Fat 4 g
Sodium 83 mg
Cholesterol 5 mg

Sweet Potatoes over Rice

1 pound sweet potatoes, peeled
1 tablespoon vegetable oil
1 small onion, chopped
1 clove garlic, minced
1 cup coconut milk
½ cup frozen green peas, thawed
2 cups hot cooked basmati rice (or other white rice)
2 tablespoons chopped fresh cilantro

Cut sweet potatoes into ½-inch chunks. Cover with water, and heat to boiling. Cook over medium heat until tender. Heat oil in skillet. Add onion and garlic. Sauté until tender. Add coconut milk, drained sweet potatoes, and peas. Simmer 10 to 15 minutes to blend flavors. Place hot rice on plates. Top with potato mixture. Sprinkle with cilantro before serving.

Makes 4 servings.

One serving = 2 starches + 2 fats
Calories per serving = 271
Protein 4 g
Carbohydrates 36 g
Fat 13 g
Sodium 69 mg
Cholesterol 0 mg

Quinoa with Apricots and Pecans

2 cups water
1 cup quinoa
¼ cup chopped pecans, toasted
¼ cup chopped dried apricots
½ cup chopped onion
¼ cup raspberry vinaigrette salad dressing

Boil water in medium saucepan. Stir in quinoa. Cover, reduce heat, and simmer 10 minutes. Turn off heat source and leave on burner, covered, for 20 minutes until water is absorbed. Pour quinoa into large mixing bowl. While quinoa is still warm, stir in pecans, apricots, onion, and salad dressing. Toss to mix; serve either warm or cool.

Makes 4 servings.

One serving = 1 starch + 1 fruit + 2 fats
Calories per serving = 330
Protein 11 g
Carbohydrates 34 g
Fat 12 g
Sodium 58 mg
Cholesterol 0 mg

Pineapple Rice

2 cups water
1 teaspoon olive oil
½ teaspoon salt
1 cup long-grain white rice
1 8-ounce can crushed pineapple
½ cup frozen peas
2 scallions or green onions, chopped

Combine water, olive oil, salt, and rice in saucepan.
Cook over medium heat 15 to 20 minutes, or until liquid is absorbed.
Add pineapple, peas, and green onions.
Cook until peas are tender, about 5 minutes longer.

Makes 4 servings.

One serving = 2 starches
Calories per serving = 174
Protein 4 g
Carbohydrates 36 g
Fat 2 g
Sodium 58 mg
Cholesterol 0 mg

Orange and Basil Black Beans

2 cups cooked black beans or canned black beans, rinsed and drained
½ cup peeled, seeded, and chopped cucumber
½ cup seeded and chopped plum tomatoes
½ cup thinly sliced celery
2 tablespoons finely chopped fresh basil leaves
½ cup mandarin orange sections
3 tablespoons low-fat vinaigrette salad dressing

Combine all ingredients in bowl. Toss gently.
Let stand 30 to 60 minutes for flavors to blend before serving.

Makes 4 servings.

One serving = 1 starch + 1 lean meat + 1 vegetable
Calories per serving = 171
Protein 11 g
Carbohydrates 18 g
Fat 4 g
Sodium 272 mg
Cholesterol 0 mg

Red Lentil Hash

1½ cups dried red lentils, rinsed and drained
3½ cups water
1 carrot, shredded
1 small zucchini, shredded
½ red bell pepper, diced
1 green onion, chopped fine
1 teaspoon grated fresh gingerroot or ¼ teaspoon ground ginger
¼ cup balsamic vinaigrette salad dressing

In large saucepan, bring lentils and water to a boil. Reduce heat to simmer. Cook 10 minutes. Add carrot, zucchini, red pepper, green onion, ginger, and salad dressing. Cover and cook 3 to 5 minutes longer. Remove from heat. Let stand 5 minutes before serving.

Makes 4 servings.

One serving = 2 starches + 1 lean meat
Calories per serving = 247
Protein 15 g
Carbohydrates 57 g
Fat 4 g
Sodium 216 mg
Cholesterol 0 mg

Mushroom–Barley Stew

1 pound fresh mushrooms
¼ cup olive oil or vegetable oil
1 medium onion, peeled and chopped
2 cloves garlic, peeled and chopped
2 stalks celery, diced
2 carrots, peeled and chopped
1 quart water
1 cup barley
¼ cup chopped fresh parsley
Salt and pepper to taste

Wash and thinly slice mushrooms. Heat oil in large saucepan; add mushrooms, onion, and garlic. Sauté until soft. Add celery, carrots, water, and barley. Heat to boiling, stirring frequently. Lower heat, and simmer, covered, until barley is tender, about 30 to 40 minutes. Just before serving, sprinkle with parsley, and season with salt and pepper.

Makes 6 servings.

One serving = 2 starches + 1 lean meat + 1 vegetable
Calories per serving = 241
Protein 14 g
Carbohydrates 41 g
Fat 4 g
Sodium (with no salt added) 187 mg
Cholesterol 0 mg

Curried Lentil Stew

1 teaspoon olive oil
½ cup chopped onion
1 carrot, peeled and chopped
1 to 2 teaspoons curry powder
2 bay leaves
2 cups water
1 14-ounce can whole tomatoes
½ cup lentils, rinsed and drained
1 cup diced potatoes
Salt and pepper to taste

Heat oil in large saucepan over medium heat. Add onion, carrot, curry
powder, bay leaves, water, tomatoes, lentils, and potatoes.
Bring to boil; reduce heat and simmer 25 to 30 minutes, covered.
When lentils are tender, remove from heat, and season with salt and pepper.

Makes 4 servings.

One serving = 2 starches + 1 very lean meat
Calories per serving = 160
Protein 9 g
Carbohydrates 27 g
Fat 1 g
Sodium 371 mg
Cholesterol 0 mg

Black Bean Soup

1 15-ounce can black beans, undrained
1 medium onion, chopped
1 clove garlic, minced
½ teaspoon ground cumin
2 fresh tomatoes, seeded and chopped
2 tablespoons chopped fresh cilantro
Salt and pepper to taste

Combine beans, onion, garlic, cumin, and tomatoes in large saucepan. Cook 15 to 20 minutes over medium heat until onion is tender. Stir occasionally, and add water as needed to prevent sticking. Remove from heat. Cool. Puree half of soup in blender or food processor until smooth, and return it to saucepan. If soup is too thick, add water to desired consistency. Reheat soup. Sprinkle with cilantro, salt, and pepper just before serving.

Makes 4 servings.

One serving = 1 starch
Calories per serving = 92
Protein 4 g
Carbohydrates 11 g
Fat 1 g
Sodium (no salt added) 67 mg
Cholesterol 0 mg

Mexican Eggs

1 tablespoon vegetable oil
¼ cup chopped onion
1 clove garlic, minced
½ cup frozen corn, thawed
¼ teaspoon ground cumin
2 eggs, slightly beaten
½ cup unsalted corn chips

Heat oil in large skillet; add onion and garlic. Sauté over medium heat until onion is tender. Add corn, cumin, and eggs. Stir until eggs are set. Arrange corn chips on plate. Spoon egg mixture on chips. Serve immediately.

Makes 2 servings.

One serving = 1 medium-fat meat + 2 starches + 1 fat
Calories per serving = 266
Protein 9 g
Carbohydrates 29 g
Fat 7 g
Sodium 87 mg
Cholesterol 213 mg

Veggie Roll-Ups

2 large flour tortillas
½ cup hummus or crumbled feta cheese
2 green onions, finely chopped
½ cup shredded lettuce
½ large cucumber, seeded and chopped

Spread tortillas with hummus, or sprinkle with cheese. Top with onions, lettuce, and cucumber. Roll up and serve.

Makes 2 servings.

One serving = 2 starches + 1 medium-fat meat + 1 vegetable
Calories per serving = 234
Protein 6 g
Carbohydrates 31 g
Fat 7 g
Sodium 159 mg
Cholesterol (with feta cheese) 19 mg

Easy Veggie Pizza

4 small whole-grain pita bread rounds (or English muffin halves)
1 cup small pieces of assorted vegetables such as broccoli, cauliflower, chopped green bell pepper, sliced mushrooms
¼ cup pizza sauce
1 cup (2 ounces) shredded low-fat Mozzarella cheese

Preheat oven to 400°F. Place pita bread rounds on baking sheet. Bake 5 minutes. Meanwhile, steam vegetables just until tender. Spread pizza sauce on bread. Sprinkle with vegetables, and top with cheese. Bake 10 to 12 minutes, or until cheese is melted and edges are brown.

Makes 4 servings.

One serving = 1 starch + 1 vegetable + 1 medium-fat meat
Calories per serving = 206
Protein 10 g
Carbohydrates 24 g
Fat 7 g
Sodium 318 mg
Cholesterol 36 mg

South of the Border Pizza

1 whole wheat English muffin, split in half
¼ cup mild or hot salsa
2 green onions, chopped fine
½ green bell pepper, chopped fine
¼ cup shredded low-fat Monterey Jack or cheddar cheese

Place muffin halves on toaster oven rack or baking sheet.
Spread salsa on each muffin half. Top with onions and green pepper.
Sprinkle cheese evenly over muffin halves.
Toast in toaster oven or broil in conventional oven until cheese melts.

Makes 1 serving.

One serving = 2 starches + 2 medium-fat meats + 1 vegetable
Calories per serving = 303
Protein 23 g
Carbohydrates 38 g
Fat 11 g
Sodium 671 mg
Cholesterol 108 mg

Roasted Asparagus with Rosemary

1 teaspoon olive oil
14 thin fresh asparagus spears
2 small garlic cloves, minced
1 tablespoon fresh rosemary leaves or 1 teaspoon dried rosemary

Preheat oven to 425°F. Combine oil, asparagus, garlic, and rosemary in baking pan. Toss gently to coat each spear of asparagus.
Roast uncovered 10 minutes, or until asparagus is tender.

Makes 2 servings.

One serving = 1 vegetable
Calories per serving = 32
Protein 2 g
Carbohydrates 6 g
Fat 3 g
Sodium 42 mg
Cholesterol 0 mg

Asparagus and Pistachio Risotto

¼ cup olive oil

1 small onion, chopped fine

2 cups arborio rice

4 to 4½ cups water

½ pound fresh thin asparagus spears, cut into 1-inch pieces

¼ cup whipping cream

½ cup grated Parmesan cheese

¼ cup shelled, chopped pistachios

Heat oil in saucepan. Add onion and sauté until onion is soft, about 3 minutes. Add rice and 3 cups water, stirring constantly. As liquid is absorbed, add additional 1 to 1½ cups water and continue cooking until rice is tender. Add asparagus. Remove from heat. Stir in cream and cheese. Just before serving, sprinkle with nuts.

Makes 4 servings.

One serving = 2 starches + 1 fat + 1 medium-fat meat + 1 vegetable

Calories per serving = 316

Protein 14 g

Carbohydrates 37 g

Fat 12 g

Sodium 121 mg

Cholesterol 94 mg

Roasted Asparagus Parmesan

1 pound asparagus spears
1 tablespoon olive oil
¼ cup grated Parmesan cheese

Preheat oven to 400°F. Lay asparagus spears on lightly oiled cookie sheet.
Drizzle with olive oil. Sprinkle with cheese.
Roast 10 minutes, or until asparagus is tender.

Makes 4 servings.

One serving = 1 vegetable + 1 fat + ½ medium-fat meat
Calories per serving = 94
Protein 4 g
Carbohydrates 6 g
Fat 9 g
Sodium 79 mg
Cholesterol 27 mg

Green Bean and Cherry Tomato Casserole

1 pound fresh green beans

1 small red onion, sliced thin

2 teaspoons olive oil

2 teaspoons balsamic vinegar

12 cherry tomatoes, cut in half

1 tablespoon fresh thyme leaves or 1 teaspoon dried thyme

Steam green beans just till tender. Combine beans, onion, olive oil, vinegar, tomatoes, and thyme in skillet. Sauté about 2 minutes, stirring constantly. Serve immediately.

Makes 2 servings.

One serving = 2 vegetables + 1 fat

Calories per serving = 66

Protein 2 g

Carbohydrates 8 g

Fat 6 g

Sodium 37 mg

Cholesterol 0 mg

Marinated Broccoli

1 pound broccoli, cut into serving pieces
1 2-inch piece fresh gingerroot
½ cup low-fat honey-mustard salad dressing

Steam broccoli until tender. Place in shallow glass casserole dish. Grate ginger, and sprinkle over broccoli. Pour salad dressing over broccoli. Cover. Refrigerate at least 1 hour before serving.

Makes 4 servings.

One serving = 1 vegetable + 1 fat
Calories per serving = 34
Protein 2 g
Carbohydrates 4 g
Fat 6 g
Sodium 291 mg
Cholesterol 0 mg

Hot German Cabbage

1 tablespoon margarine or butter
2 cups shredded red cabbage
1 apple, chopped
½ small onion, chopped
2 teaspoons sugar
½ teaspoon caraway seeds
¼ teaspoon dry mustard
2 tablespoons red wine vinegar

Melt margarine in large skillet. Sauté cabbage, apple, and onion in skillet over medium heat until apple is tender. Add sugar, caraway seeds, mustard, and vinegar. Simmer until cabbage is tender, about 5 minutes.

Makes 2 servings.

One serving = 1 vegetable + 1 fruit + 1 fat
Calories per serving = 101
Protein 1 g
Carbohydrates 13 g
Fat 4 g
Sodium 18 mg
Cholesterol (with margarine) 0 mg
Cholesterol (with butter) 5 mg

Stir-Fried Collards

1 bunch (about 1 pound) fresh collard greens
1 tablespoon vegetable oil
2 small cloves garlic, chopped fine
1 to 2 teaspoons oyster sauce
Freshly ground pepper to taste

Steam collard greens just till tender. Heat wok and add oil. Stir-fry garlic until lightly brown. Add greens and oyster sauce. Stir constantly to blend ingredients. Serve immediately with freshly ground pepper.

Makes 2 servings.

One serving = 1 vegetable + 1 fat
Calories per serving = 51
Protein 1 g
Carbohydrates 4 g
Fat 7 g
Sodium 67 mg
Cholesterol 0 mg

Herb-Roasted Potatoes

2 pounds small red potatoes
2 tablespoons olive oil
4 tablespoons chopped fresh basil leaves or 2 tablespoons dried basil
½ teaspoon salt

Preheat oven to 400°F. Wash potatoes, and cut into quarters. Put potato wedges in bowl, and add olive oil, basil, and salt. Toss gently to coat potato wedges evenly with oil mixture. Pour onto baking sheet. Bake 30 to 40 minutes, or until edges of potatoes are brown and crisp.

Makes 4 servings.

One serving = 1 starch + 1 fat
Calories per serving = 146
Protein 1 g
Carbohydrates 21 g
Fat 4 g
Sodium 301 mg
Cholesterol 0 mg

Salt-Baked Rosemary Potatoes

3 pounds kosher salt
1½ pounds fingerling potatoes
4 to 6 sprigs rosemary
Olive oil

Preheat oven to 400°F. Pour thin layer of salt in a 13″ × 9″ baking pan.
Place potatoes in single layer on top of salt. Scatter rosemary over potatoes.
Cover with remaining salt. Bake 40 to 45 minutes, or until fork-tender.
Leave potatoes in salt until ready to serve.
Just before serving, brush off salt, and drizzle with olive oil.

Makes 4 servings.

One serving = 1 starch
Calories per serving = 92
Protein 2 g
Carbohydrates 17 g
Fat 1 g (without olive oil)
Sodium 218 mg
Cholesterol 0 mg

Garlic Sautéed Spinach and Onions

1 teaspoon olive oil
1 teaspoon butter or margarine
3 cups chopped fresh spinach leaves, stems removed
1 onion, chopped
1 clove garlic, minced

Heat olive oil and butter in saucepan over medium heat. Add spinach, onion, and garlic. Sauté until spinach is limp and tender. Serve hot.

Makes 2 servings.

One serving = 1 vegetable + 1 fat
Calories per serving = 67
Protein 1 g
Carbohydrates 6 g
Fat 7 g
Sodium 31 mg
Cholesterol (with butter) 3 mg

Baked Sweet Potatoes
Stuffed with Cranberries, Pear, and Pecans

4 medium-size sweet potatoes
1 cup fresh or frozen cranberries
1 ripe pear, peeled, cored, and chopped
⅓ cup coarsely chopped pecans
1 tablespoon brown sugar

Preheat oven to 400°F. Place sweet potatoes on baking sheet. Bake until potatoes are tender when pierced with fork, about 45 minutes. Meanwhile, combine cranberries, pear, pecans, and brown sugar in saucepan. Simmer over medium heat until pears are tender and cranberries "pop." Cut open each sweet potato. Using fork, gently mash pulp inside each potato. Mound cranberry mixture into each sweet potato. Serve warm.

Makes 4 servings.

One serving = 1 starch + 1 fruit + 1 fat
Calories per serving = 191
Protein 2 g
Carbohydrates 28 g
Fat 7 g
Sodium 87 mg
Cholesterol 0 mg

Desserts

Who doesn't like dessert? Delicious desserts need not be off-limits to people with diabetes. Try these mouthwatering, easy-to-make recipes.

Pecan Pie

½ cup light corn syrup
½ cup brown sugar
½ cup no-calorie sweetener, such as Splenda
3 eggs
¼ cup margarine or butter, melted
¼ cup water
½ cup pecan halves
1 9-inch unbaked piecrust

Preheat oven to 350°F. Combine corn syrup, brown sugar, sweetener, eggs, margarine, and water in large bowl. Beat well. Pour filling into unbaked piecrust. Sprinkle with pecans. Bake 40 to 50 minutes, or until center is set (toothpick comes out clean). Cool.

Makes 10 servings.

One serving = 3 carbohydrates (or 1 starch + 2 fruits) + 3 fats
Calories per serving = 348
Protein 3 g
Carbohydrates 42 g
Fat 17 g
Sodium 90 mg
Cholesterol 206 mg

Strawberry Pizza Dessert

1 17-ounce package refrigerated sugar cookie dough
8 ounces low-fat cream cheese, softened
1/3 cup no-calorie sweetener, such as Splenda
2 cups sliced fresh strawberries
Powdered sugar

Roll out cookie dough into a round pizza pan. Bake according to directions on package. Cool. Meantime, beat cream cheese and sweetener together until fluffy. Spread over top of cooled crust. Place strawberry slices over cheese filling. Just before serving, sprinkle with powdered sugar.

Makes 12 servings.

One serving = 2 carbohydrates (or 1 starch + 1 fruit) + 2 fats
Calories per serving = 274
Protein 4 g
Carbohydrates 33 g
Fat 12 g
Sodium 128 mg
Cholesterol 18 mg

Chocolate Raspberry Cheesecake

1½ pounds (3 8-ounce packages) low-fat cream cheese, softened
1 cup no-calorie sweetener, such as Splenda
2 eggs
1 cup low-fat vanilla yogurt
⅓ cup all-purpose flour
15 no-sugar chocolate wafers
¾ cup low-sugar raspberry preserves

Preheat oven to 400°F. Combine cream cheese, sugar substitute, eggs, yogurt, and flour in mixing bowl. Beat with mixer at medium speed for about 5 minutes, or until mixture is smooth. Crush cookies in blender until they are fine crumbs; transfer to separate mixing bowl. Heat ¼ cup raspberry preserves; add to cookie crumbs. Toss together. Press crumb mixture into bottom of 8-inch springform pan. Place in freezer about 5 minutes to set. Spread remaining preserves over crust. Pour cream cheese batter over raspberry preserves. Bake 10 minutes. Reduce oven temperature to 300°F. Bake 35 minutes longer, or until center is firm. Turn oven off. Leave cheesecake in oven for another hour; remove it and let cool thoroughly. Open springform pan, and transfer cheesecake to serving platter.

Makes 16 servings.

One serving = 1 carbohydrate (or 1 starch) + 2 fats
Calories per serving = 203
Protein 7 g
Carbohydrates 17 g
Fat 12 g
Sodium 241 mg
Cholesterol 72 mg

Chocolate Kwanzaa Cake

⅔ cup butter or margarine, softened
¾ cup sugar
¾ cup no-calorie sweetener, such as Splenda
2 eggs
2 cups all-purpose flour
¾ cup cocoa powder
1½ teaspoons baking soda
2 cups (16 ounces) low-fat plain yogurt
½ cup (1 ripe) mashed banana
½ cup flaked sweetened coconut
Powdered sugar

Preheat oven to 350°F. Grease and flour Bundt cake pan. Beat together butter, sugar, sugar substitute, and eggs until creamy. Add flour, cocoa, baking soda, and yogurt. Mix well. Stir in banana and coconut. Pour batter into prepared cake pan. Bake 55 to 60 minutes, or until wooden toothpick inserted into center comes out clean. Cool 10 minutes on wire rack. Invert and remove cake from pan. Cool thoroughly. Just before serving, sprinkle with powdered sugar.

Makes 12 servings.

One serving = 3 carbohydrates (or 1 starch + 2 fruits) + 2 fats
Calories per serving = 256
Protein 4 g
Carbohydrates 41 g
Fat 13 g
Sodium 241 mg
Cholesterol 174 mg

German Chocolate Cake

Unsweetened cocoa powder
¼ cup flaked coconut
1 box (18¼ ounces) German chocolate cake mix
6 ounces (¾ cup) low-fat plain yogurt
½ cup water
¼ cup vegetable oil
2 large eggs

Preheat oven to 350°F. Generously grease Bundt cake pan. Dust cake pan with cocoa. Sprinkle coconut onto sides and bottom of pan. Combine cake mix, yogurt, water, oil, and eggs in large mixing bowl. Blend with electric mixer on low speed for 1 minute to moisten all ingredients. Scrape sides of bowl with spatula. Beat at medium speed for 3 minutes longer. Pour batter into prepared cake pan. Bake 30 to 40 minutes, or until cake springs back when touched in middle with your finger. Cool on rack 5 minutes. Invert cake pan to remove cake. Cool completely.

Makes 12 servings.

One serving = 2 carbohydrates (or 1 starch + 1 fruit) + 2 fats
Calories per serving = 256
Protein 3 g
Carbohydrates 39 g
Fat 12 g
Sodium 253 mg
Cholesterol 169 mg

Better than Sex Chocolate Cake

1 box (18¼ ounces) chocolate cake mix
¾ cup fat-free evaporated milk
1 6-ounce jar fat-free caramel ice-cream syrup
1 2.2-ounce crunch chocolate bar "without added sugar,"
cut into small pieces
1 8-ounce container frozen fat-free whipped topping, thawed

Bake cake in prepared 9″ × 13″ pan according to package directions. Cool on wire rack 5 minutes. With table knife, cut slits across top of cake, making sure not to go through to bottom. In saucepan over low heat, combine milk and caramel syrup. Stir until smooth. Slowly pour mixture over cake. Sprinkle surface of cake with chocolate pieces. Let cake cool completely. Cut into 15 pieces. Spoon whipped topping onto each serving.

Makes 15 servings.

One serving = 3 carbohydrates (or 1 starch + 2 fruits) + 1 fat
Calories per serving = 284
Protein 3 g
Carbohydrates 41 g
Fat 7 g
Sodium 201 mg
Cholesterol 48 mg

Root Beer Float Cake

1 box (18¼ ounces) white cake mix
1¾ cups sugar-free root beer
¼ cup vegetable oil
2 eggs
1 envelope dry whipped topping mix

Preheat oven to 350°F. Grease and flour 13″ × 9″ baking pan. Beat together cake mix, 1¼ cups root beer, vegetable oil, and eggs about 2 minutes, or until batter is smooth. Pour into baking pan. Bake 30 to 35 minutes, or until toothpick inserted into center comes out clean. Cool completely on wire rack. Prepare frosting by combining whipped topping mix and remaining ½ cup root beer in mixing bowl. Beat until stiff peaks form. Frost cake. Store in refrigerator.

Makes 12 servings.

One serving = 2 carbohydrates (or 1 starch + 1 fruit) + 2 fats
Calories per serving = 251
Protein 3 g
Carbohydrates 34 g
Fat 11 g
Sodium 297 mg
Cholesterol 59 mg

Mocha Snack Cake

1 box (18¼ ounces) chocolate cake mix
1¼ cups cold coffee
½ cup vegetable oil
3 eggs
¼ cup powdered sugar
2 teaspoons instant coffee

Preheat oven to 350°F. Lightly oil 9″ × 13″ baking pan. Beat together cake
mix, coffee, vegetable oil, and eggs about 2 minutes, or until batter is
smooth. Pour into prepared pan. Bake 30 to 35 minutes, or until toothpick
inserted into center comes out clean. Cool on wire rack at least 15 minutes.
Combine powdered sugar and instant coffee in blender. Blend to mix.
Sprinkle on top of cake.

Makes 12 servings.

One serving = 2 carbohydrates (or 1 starch + 1 fruit) + 2 fats
Calories per serving = 247
Protein 4 g
Carbohydrates 36 g
Fat 13 g
Sodium 369 mg
Cholesterol 62 mg

7-Up Cake

1 box (18¼ ounces) yellow cake mix
1 0.8-ounce box sugar-free instant vanilla pudding mix
5 eggs
½ cup vegetable oil
1 12-ounce can sugar-free 7-Up, or other sugar-free lemon-lime soda
1 cup no-calorie sweetener, such as Splenda
1 6-ounce can juice-packed crushed pineapple, undrained
½ cup shredded coconut

Preheat oven to 350°F. Lightly grease 9″ × 13″ baking pan. Combine cake mix, pudding mix, 3 eggs, and vegetable oil in mixing bowl. Beat until light and fluffy. Add 7-Up, mixing on low speed until well blended. Pour into prepared pan. Bake 40 minutes, or until toothpick inserted into center comes out clean. Make topping while cake is baking by mixing together remaining 2 eggs, sugar substitute, pineapple, and coconut. When cake is done baking, prick top all over with fork to allow topping to run through cake. Pour pineapple-coconut topping over cake. Return to oven for 5 more minutes. Cool on wire rack.

Makes 16 servings.

One serving = 2 carbohydrates (or 1 starch + 1 fruit) + 2 fats
Calories per serving = 289
Protein 5 g
Carbohydrates 39 g
Fat 13 g
Sodium 478 mg
Cholesterol 54 mg

Pumpkin–Maple Cake

1½ cups pumpkin
3 eggs
1¼ cups low-sugar syrup
1 cup sugar
1 cup vegetable oil
3 cups all-purpose flour
1 tablespoon baking powder
½ teaspoon baking soda
2 teaspoons ground cinnamon
¼ teaspoon ground cloves
Powdered sugar

Preheat oven to 350°F. Oil Bundt cake pan or 9″ × 13″ baking pan. Beat together pumpkin, eggs, syrup, sugar, and vegetable oil. Add flour, baking powder, baking soda, cinnamon, and cloves. Beat until smooth. Pour into prepared pan. Bake 35 to 40 minutes, or until toothpick inserted into center comes out clean. Cool on wire rack 10 minutes. Remove from pan. When completely cool, sprinkle with powdered sugar.

Makes 16 servings.

One serving = 2 carbohydrates (or 1 starch + 1 fruit) + 2 fats
Calories per serving = 261
Protein 3 g
Carbohydrates 37 g
Fat 12 g
Sodium 127 mg
Cholesterol 61 mg

Blueberry Loaf Cake

1 cup margarine or butter
1 cup no-calorie sweetener, such as Splenda
4 eggs
1 teaspoon pure vanilla extract
¼ teaspoon ground nutmeg
1½ cups all-purpose flour
2 teaspoons baking powder
1 cup fresh blueberries

Preheat oven to 350°F. Lightly oil and flour a 9″ × 5″ loaf pan. In large
bowl, beat together margarine, sugar substitute, eggs, and vanilla.
Add nutmeg, flour, and baking powder. Beat until well blended.
Gently stir in blueberries. Pour into prepared pan. Bake 50 to 60 minutes,
or until toothpick inserted into cake center comes out clean.
Cool on wire rack 10 minutes; remove from pan.

Makes 12 servings.

One serving = 1 starch + 2 fats
Calories per serving = 197
Protein 4 g
Carbohydrates 19 g
Fat 13 g
Sodium 42 mg
Cholesterol 59 mg

Banana Cake

1 box (18¼ ounces) yellow cake mix
½ cup vegetable oil
3 eggs
1 cup water
1 teaspoon ground cinnamon
2 ripe bananas, mashed
Powdered sugar

Preheat oven to 350°F. Lightly oil and flour 13″ × 9″ baking pan. Prepare cake mix according to package directions, using the vegetable oil, eggs, and water. Add cinnamon and bananas. Mix well. Pour batter into prepared pan. Bake 35 to 40 minutes, or until toothpick inserted into center comes out clean. Remove from oven and cool on wire rack.
Just before serving, dust with powdered sugar.

Makes 16 servings.

One serving = 2 carbohydrates + 2 fats
Calories per serving = 277
Protein 4 g
Carbohydrates 42 g
Fat 12 g
Sodium 291 mg
Cholesterol 34 mg

Peanut Butter Cupcakes

1 box (18¼ ounces) yellow cake mix
2 eggs
⅓ cup creamy peanut butter
3 tablespoons vegetable oil
1½ cups low-fat milk
Powdered sugar

Preheat oven to 350°F. Line muffin pan with paper baking cups. Beat cake
mix, eggs, peanut butter, vegetable oil, and milk at medium speed
2 minutes. When batter is smooth, pour into muffin cups. Bake 15 to
20 minutes, or until toothpick inserted into center comes out clean.
Cool completely, and remove from pan.
Just before serving, sprinkle with powdered sugar.

Makes 24 cupcakes.

One cupcake = 2 carbohydrates (or 1 starch + 1 fruit) + 2 fats
Calories per serving = 269
Protein 6 g
Carbohydrates 37 g
Fat 14 g
Sodium 457 mg
Cholesterol 62 mg

Double Chocolate Cupcakes

1 box (18¼ ounces) devil's food cake mix
1 cup water
3 eggs
⅓ cup vegetable oil
½ cup semisweet chocolate pieces
2 tablespoons unsweetened cocoa powder
¼ cup no-calorie sweetener, such as Splenda

Preheat oven to 350°F. Line muffin pan with paper baking cups. Prepare cake mix according to package directions, using the water, eggs, and vegetable oil. When batter is smooth, stir in chocolate pieces. Pour into cupcake pan. Bake 12 to 15 minutes, or until toothpick inserted into center comes out clean. Cool. Mix together cocoa and sugar substitute. Sprinkle on cupcakes.

Makes 24 cupcakes.

One cupcake = 2 carbohydrates (or 1 starch + 1 fruit) + 2 fats
Calories per serving = 281
Protein 3 g
Carbohydrates 31 g
Fat 13 g
Sodium 237 mg
Cholesterol 32 mg

Chewy Nugget Bars

3 tablespoons butter or margarine
⅓ pound marshmallows
4 cups cornflakes
½ cup flaked coconut
⅓ cup chopped walnuts
½ cup semisweet chocolate chips, melted

Oil an 8-inch square baking pan. In large saucepan, melt butter and
marshmallows over low heat, stirring constantly. Remove from heat.
Fold in cereal, coconut, and walnuts. Spread into prepared pan.
Pat mixture evenly into pan. Drizzle chocolate over top.
Chill until firm, and cut into 2-inch squares.

Makes 16 squares.

One square = 3 carbohydrates (or 1 starch + 2 fruits) + 2 fats
Calories per serving = 272
Protein 2 g
Carbohydrates 38 g
Fat 12 g
Sodium 174 mg
Cholesterol 18 mg

Lemon Yogurt Bars

1 17-ounce package refrigerated sugar cookie dough
1½ teaspoons baking powder
¼ cup no-calorie sweetener, such as Splenda
2 eggs
6 ounces (¾ cup) low-fat lemon yogurt
Powdered sugar

Preheat oven according to cookie dough package. Press cookie dough into bottom of 9″ × 13″ baking pan. Bake 12 to 15 minutes, or until browned. For topping, combine baking powder, sugar substitute, eggs, and yogurt in mixing bowl. Beat well. Pour evenly over baked crust. Bake another 15 to 20 minutes until top is crispy and set. Cool in pan on wire rack. Cut into 24 bars. Before serving, sprinkle with powdered sugar.

Makes 24 bars.

One bar = 2 carbohydrates (or 1 starch + 1 fruit) + 2 fats
Calories per serving = 297
Protein 4 g
Carbohydrates 31 g
Fat 13 g
Sodium 210 mg
Cholesterol 84 mg

Chocolate Brownies

½ cup sugar
½ cup no-calorie sweetener, such as Splenda
2 eggs
½ cup vegetable oil
2 ounces unsweetened chocolate, melted
1½ cups all-purpose flour
1 teaspoon baking soda

Preheat oven to 350°F. Lightly oil 9″ × 13″ baking pan. Beat together sugar,
sugar substitute, eggs, vegetable oil, and chocolate until light and fluffy.
Add flour and baking soda. Mix well. Pour into prepared pan.
Bake 25 to 30 minutes, or until center is firm. *Do not overbake.*
Cool in pan on wire rack. Cut into 16 bars.

Makes 16 brownies.

One brownie = 2 carbohydrates (or 1 starch + 1 fruit) + 2 fats
Calories per serving = 249
Protein 3 g
Carbohydrates 34 g
Fat 12 g
Sodium 291 mg
Cholesterol 33 mg

Chewy Chocolate Gingerbread Cookies

1½ cups all-purpose flour

1 teaspoon baking soda

1 teaspoon ground ginger

¼ teaspoon ground cloves

¼ teaspoon ground nutmeg

½ cup margarine or butter, softened

⅓ cup dark brown sugar

¼ cup molasses

2 eggs

1 cup semisweet chocolate pieces

Mix flour, baking soda, ginger, cloves, and nutmeg in bowl. In separate mixing bowl, beat together margarine, brown sugar, molasses, and eggs about 4 minutes until well combined. Mix in flour mixture and chocolate pieces. Spread dough onto waxed paper or plastic wrap. Shape dough into 1-inch roll. Seal paper around dough. Refrigerate until firm, 2 hours or more. When ready to bake, preheat oven to 350°F. Pinch off enough dough to make 1½-inch diameter balls. Place about 2 inches apart on lightly greased cookie sheet. Bake 10 to 12 minutes, or until dough surface cracks. Cool 5 minutes on pan before transferring to wire rack to finish cooling.

Makes 24 cookies.

One cookie = 2 carbohydrates (or 1 starch + 1 fruit) + 2 fats

Calories per serving = 256

Protein 2 g

Carbohydrates 39 g

Fat 13 g

Sodium 55 mg

Cholesterol (with margarine) 0 mg

Cholesterol (with butter) 7 mg

Sugar-Free Chocolate Chip Cookies

1 cup all-purpose flour
½ teaspoon baking soda
½ teaspoon baking powder
½ cup vegetable oil
½ cup no-calorie sweetener, such as Splenda
1 egg
½ cup semisweet chocolate pieces

Preheat oven to 375°F. Combine flour, baking soda, and baking powder in bowl. Beat in oil, sugar substitute, and egg. Mix well. Stir in chocolate pieces. Drop by teaspoonfuls onto lightly oiled cookie sheet. Bake 10 to 12 minutes, or until browned. Remove from oven and cool on wire rack.

Makes 18 cookies.

One cookie = 1 starch + 1 fat
Calories per serving = 136
Protein 2 g
Carbohydrates 19 g
Fat 8 g
Sodium 71 mg
Cholesterol 14 mg

Peanut Butter Oatmeal Cookies

½ cup vegetable oil
½ cup creamy peanut butter
½ cup sugar
1 egg
1 cup all-purpose flour
½ teaspoon baking soda
¾ cup quick-cooking rolled oats

Preheat oven to 375°F. Beat together oil, peanut butter, sugar, and egg. Add flour, baking soda, and oats, and beat well. Drop by rounded teaspoonfuls about 2 inches apart on lightly oiled cookie sheet. Bake in oven 8 to 10 minutes, or until edges are golden. Cool on wire rack.

Makes 36 cookies.

One cookie = 1 starch + 2 fats
Calories per serving = 192
Protein 3 g
Carbohydrates 19 g
Fat 14 g
Sodium 264 mg
Cholesterol 16 mg

Tiramisu

3 eggs, separated
½ cup sugar
1 cup mascarpone cheese or 8 ounces low-fat cream cheese
1 cup espresso
3 ounces ladyfingers
Grated semisweet chocolate

Combine egg yolks and sugar in medium saucepan over *low* heat. Beat with whip until thick and lemon colored. Cook 5 to 8 minutes, stirring constantly. Remove from heat. Add cheese. Beat until smooth. Cool thoroughly. Meanwhile, beat egg whites until so stiff you can turn bowl on its side and they don't move. Fold into cheese mixture. Dip sugared side of ladyfingers halfway into espresso. Lay half the ladyfingers in single layer in bottom of 8-inch square glass dish or trifle bowl. Spread on half the cheese mixture. Repeat ladyfinger layer. Spread with remaining cheese mixture. Sprinkle with grated chocolate. Refrigerate 2 hours or overnight before serving.

Makes 8 servings.

One serving = 3 carbohydrates (or 1 starch + 2 fruits) + 2 fats
Calories per serving = 284
Protein 5 g
Carbohydrates 41 g
Fat 13 g
Sodium 167 mg
Cholesterol 188 mg

Coconut Cream Pudding

1 0.8-ounce box sugar-free vanilla pudding mix
2 cups coconut milk
¼ cup flaked coconut

Prepare pudding according to package directions, using coconut milk.
Before pouring pudding into serving dishes, stir in flaked coconut.
Serve warm or chilled.

Makes 4 servings.

One serving = 3 fats
Calories per serving = 227
Protein 1 g
Carbohydrates 2 g
Fat 18 g
Sodium 18 mg
Cholesterol 0 mg

Rice Pudding

⅓ **cup rice**
⅓ **cup sugar**
4 cups low-fat milk
Pinch saffron
Cinnamon stick

Preheat oven to 325°F. Mix together all ingredients in 3- to 4-quart
casserole or ovenproof casserole dish. Bake 30 minutes. Stir.
Bake 30 minutes longer. Rice kernels will begin to enlarge in mixture.
Stir. Continue baking 10 to 15 minutes longer. Stir gently.
Remove from oven when rice kernels are swollen.
Pudding will thicken as it cools.

Makes 4 servings.

One serving = 1 starch + 1 fruit + 1 low-fat milk
Calories per serving = 241
Protein 9 g
Carbohydrates 44 g
Fat 7 g
Sodium 157 mg
Cholesterol 34 mg

Grapefruit Baked with Chocolate

1 pink or white grapefruit, at room temperature
1 tablespoon mini semisweet chocolate pieces
2 fresh strawberries
Powdered sugar

Preheat oven to 350°F. Slice grapefruit in half crosswise. Cut around grapefruit sections to loosen them and remove seeds. Sprinkle grapefruit with chocolate pieces. Place on baking pan. Bake uncovered about 5 minutes, or until chocolate softens. Remove from oven. Just before serving, top each half with a strawberry, and dust with powdered sugar.

Makes 2 servings.

One serving = 1½ fruits + 1 fat
Calories per serving = 138
Protein 1 g
Carbohydrates 26 g
Fat 4 g
Sodium 0 mg
Cholesterol 0 mg

Fruit Surprise Dessert

1 cup fresh seedless grapes, halved
1 cup fresh blueberries
1 cup fresh strawberries, halved
1 cup chopped fresh peaches
¼ cup brown sugar
2 cups low-fat vanilla yogurt

In shallow 9″ × 12″ glass dish, combine grapes, blueberries, strawberries, and peaches; mix gently. Sprinkle brown sugar over fruit. Top with yogurt. Cover and refrigerate 2 to 3 hours or overnight.
To serve, gently stir fruit and spoon into sherbet glasses.

Makes 4 servings.

One serving = 2 fruits + ½ milk
Calories per serving = 176
Protein 5 g
Carbohydrates 27 g
Fat 4 g
Sodium 147 mg
Cholesterol 22 mg

Berries Macedonia (Fruit Compote)

½ cup blueberries

½ cup blackberries

½ cup raspberries

12 fresh or frozen sweet cherries

2 ripe nectarines, cut into bite-size pieces

1 cup white wine or apple juice

1 tablespoon sambuca (anise liqueur) or 2 teaspoons pure brandy extract

Combine all ingredients in mixing bowl. Toss gently. Cover and refrigerate 2 to 4 hours. Serve in wineglasses or compote dishes.

Makes 4 servings.

One serving = 2 fruits

Calories per serving = 143

Protein 1 g

Carbohydrates 24 g

Fat 0 g

Sodium 18 mg

Cholesterol 0 mg

Bananas Flambé with Frozen Yogurt

4 small, ripe bananas, peeled
1 tablespoon margarine or butter
1 tablespoon brown sugar
½ teaspoon ground cinnamon
½ to 1 teaspoon pure rum extract
2 cups low-fat frozen yogurt

Cut bananas into slices. Melt margarine in skillet over medium heat.
Add banana slices, sugar, and cinnamon. Sauté until bananas are browned,
4 to 5 minutes. Remove from heat. Stir in rum extract.
Divide warm bananas and sauce equally among 4 dessert dishes.
Top each serving with ½ cup frozen yogurt.

Makes 4 servings.

One serving = ½ low-fat milk + 2 fruits + 1 fat
Calories per serving = 194
Protein 3 g
Carbohydrates 28 g
Fat 6 g
Sodium 89 mg
Cholesterol 15 mg

Tropical Macedonia

1 cup water

½ cup firmly packed fresh mint leaves

½ cup no-calorie sweetener, such as Splenda

4 cups peeled and cubed tropical fruits—mango, papaya,
pineapple, cherimoya

1 banana, sliced thick

1 teaspoon pure rum extract

Simmer water and mint leaves together in saucepan 20 to 30 minutes to
extract flavor. Cool. Stir in sugar substitute until dissolved. Add fruit and rum
extract. Toss gently. Cover and refrigerate 2 to 3 hours before serving.

Makes 4 servings.

One serving = 1 fruit

Calories per serving = 48

Protein 1 g

Carbohydrates 13 g

Fat 1 g

Sodium 17 mg

Cholesterol 0 mg

Apple and Cranberry Compote

1 cup diced apples
1 cup fresh or frozen cranberries
¼ cup raisins
½ teaspoon ground cinnamon
½ teaspoon pure brandy extract
2 to 3 packages sugar substitute (to taste)

Combine apples, cranberries, raisins, and cinnamon in saucepan. Cook over low heat until fruit is soft, 10 to 12 minutes. Stir occasionally to prevent burning. Add small amounts of water if fruit mixture starts to stick. Remove from heat when fruit is soft, and stir in brandy extract and sugar substitute.

Makes 4 servings.

One serving = 1 fruit
Calories per serving = 93
Protein 1 g
Carbohydrates 18 g
Fat 0 g
Sodium 4 mg
Cholesterol 0 mg

Cherry Cobbler

⅓ cup sugar
2 tablespoons margarine or butter, softened
½ cup all-purpose flour
½ teaspoon baking powder
½ teaspoon ground cinnamon
¼ cup low-fat milk
2½ cups fresh sweet cherries, pitted

Preheat oven to 350°F. Beat sugar, margarine, flour, baking powder, cinnamon, and milk in mixing bowl. Place cherries in lightly oiled 9-inch square baking pan. Spread flour mixture over cherries. Bake 25 to 30 minutes, or until crust is brown. Serve warm.

Makes 4 servings.

One serving = 2 carbohydrates (or 1 starch + 1 fruit) + 1 fat
Calories per serving = 218
Protein 3 g
Carbohydrates 41 g
Fat 8 g
Sodium 203 mg
Cholesterol 15 mg

Apple Crisp

4 cups peeled, cored, and sliced apples
3 tablespoons sugar
¼ teaspoon ground cinnamon
1 tablespoon pure brandy extract
½ cup ready-to-eat granola

Preheat oven to 375°F. Combine apples, sugar, cinnamon, and brandy extract in mixing bowl. Toss to mix thoroughly. Pour into lightly oiled 8-inch square baking pan. Sprinkle with granola.
Bake 25 to 30 minutes, or until apples are tender.

Makes 4 servings.

One serving = 2 carbohydrates (or 1 starch + 1 fruit) + 1 fat
Calories per serving = 234
Protein 5 g
Carbohydrates 29 g
Fat 7 g
Sodium 241 mg
Cholesterol 0 mg

Appendix

Carbohydrate Counting
and Food Exchanges

Carbohydrate counting is a key to determining how high and how fast your blood-glucose level will go up after eating. The carbohydrate level in foods affects your blood glucose more than the protein and fat content. Carbohydrates are found in many foods:

- Breads, cereals, and crackers
- Pasta, rice, and grains
- Vegetables
- Milk and yogurt
- Fruit and juice
- Table sugar, honey, syrup, and molasses

For better blood glucose management, space carbohydrate intake throughout the day. Another important practice is to keep portion sizes consistent. That helps you eat about the same amount of carbohydrates about the same time each day. Many people prefer carbohydrate counting to food exchanges; they find it a simpler meal-planning guide. Start with this rule of thumb:

1 carbohydrate choice = 15 grams carbohydrates

More specifically, one carbohydrate choice equals 1 starch (15 grams carbohydrates) or 1 fruit (15 grams carbohydrates) or 1 milk (12 grams carbohydrates). If you use insulin to manage your blood glucose, you can calculate your insulin dose by using the equivalent of 1 unit fast-acting insulin for each 10 to 15 grams of carbohydrates.

Sick Day Menus

During illness, diabetes can quickly get out of control. Fever, dehydration, infection, and the stress of illness can cause blood glucose levels to rise, probably due to the release of stress hormones (glucagon and cortisol).

Meal plans are particularly important for those taking insulin or oral hypoglycemic agents because food needs to be taken periodically to prevent possible hypoglycemia. Even those having dental procedures (new dentures, oral surgery, extractions) and gastrointestinal distress should monitor their blood glucose at least three to four times a day. If the blood glucose is over 240 milligrams per deciliter, test for ketones in the urine.

If the ill person with diabetes cannot tolerate regular foods, replace carbohydrates in the meal plan with liquid, semiliquid, or soft foods. The kind of carbohydrate is not the major concern. It is more important to find a food that can be tolerated, including sugar-containing liquids like soft drinks and fruit juices. A good rule of thumb is that every one to two hours, the person needs to consume 15 grams of carbohydrates (½ cup fruit juice, ½ cup applesauce, 1 cup soup, or 10 saltine crackers).

For hydration, 8 to 12 ounces of fluid (water, broth, tea) should be consumed per hour. If the person experiences vomiting and diarrhea, salted foods and liquids may be necessary to replace electrolytes.

Dietary Supplements

According to a 2001 report in the *Archives of Internal Medicine*, more than 135 million Americans indicate they use dietary supplements. In addition, scientific studies continue to demonstrate the importance of balanced, optimal nutrient intake. Today's lifestyle and eating habits often result in "unbalanced" diets that are lacking in some essential nutrients. Biochemically speaking, each person is unique and has unique nutritional needs. However, a simple, cost-effective evaluation of those individual needs is unfortunately still not available. The best insurance policy for good health in diabetes nutrition management involves the following combination of supplements:

- Take a high-quality multivitamin and mineral supplement.
- Consider including herbal products and minerals that have been shown to help control blood glucose—*Gymnema sylvestre*, *Bitter melon*, fenugreek, *Garcinia cambogia*, chromium picolinate, and vanadium.
- Add 200 to 600 milligrams of alpha lipoic acid daily as an antioxidant to increase insulin sensitivity, decrease insulin resistance, and protect against nerve damage.

The table suggests some other nutrient supplements for you to consider. Before adding them to your daily regime, discuss them with your health care provider.

Nutrient Supplements

Vitamin/ Supplement	Maximum Daily Dosage	Special Considerations
Capsaicin cream	4 applications per day	Allow 3 days to 4 weeks for results of pain reduction.
Chromium	400–800 mcg	
Fenugreek	5–30 g, 3 times per day	Seeds may be sprouted and used on salads.
Ginseng	200 mg	Not for use by those with high blood pressure. Use for 2–3 weeks, followed by a break of 1–2 weeks.
Magnesium	2 daily dosages of 400 mg each	
Quercetin	100 mg 3 times per day	
Vitamin B₆	Up to 100 mg	Avoid supplements larger than 100 mg. Best taken in form of P5P (pyridoxal 5 phosphate).
Vitamin C	250–1,000 mg	
Vitamin E	400–800 IU	

Exchange Lists for Meal Planning

The American Diabetes Association and the American Dietetic Association have produced exchange lists to aid in meal planning. They group foods together based on their similarities in carbohydrate, protein, and fat content. The lists indicate serving sizes for each stated food.

The following lists include some of the most popular foods listed in *Exchange Lists for Meal Planning 2003*. Use these lists as a reference in assessing how to use the menus and recipes from this book in your own diabetic meal plan.

Starches

One starch exchange contains about 15 grams of carbohydrates, 3 grams of protein, up to 1 gram of fat, and 80 calories per serving. In general, one starch exchange is equivalent to any of the following servings:

- ½ cup cooked cereal, grain, or starchy vegetable
- ⅓ cup cooked rice or pasta
- 1 ounce of a bread product (1 slice bread)
- ¾ to 1 ounce of most snack foods

Bread

Food Item	Serving Size
Bagel, 4 ounces	¼ (1 ounce)
Bread, reduced-calorie	2 slices (1½ ounces)
Bread, white, whole wheat, pumpernickel, or rye	1 slice (1 ounce)
Breadsticks, crisp, 4″ × ½″	4 (⅔ ounce)
English muffin	½
Hot dog bun or hamburger bun	½ (1 ounce)
Naan, 8″ × 2″	¼
Pancake, 4 inches across, ¼ inch thick	1
Pita, 6 inches across	½
Roll, plain, small	1 (1 ounce)
Raisin bread, unfrosted	1 slice (1 ounce)
Tortilla, corn or flour, 6 inches across	1
Tortilla, flour, 10 inches across	⅓
Waffle, 4 inches across, reduced-fat	1

Cereals and Grains

Food Item	Serving Size
Bran cereals	½ cup
Bulgur, cooked	½ cup

continued

Cereals and Grains, *continued*

Food Item	Serving Size
Cereals, cooked	½ cup
Cereals, unsweetened, ready-to-eat	¾ cup
Cornmeal (dry)	3 tablespoons
Couscous, cooked	⅓ cup
Flour (dry)	3 tablespoons
Granola, low-fat	¼ cup
Grape-Nuts	¼ cup
Grits	½ cup
Kasha	½ cup
Millet, cooked	⅓ cup
Muesli	¼ cup
Oats, cooked	½ cup
Pasta, cooked	⅓ cup
Puffed cereal	1 ½ cups
Rice, white or brown, cooked	⅓ cup
Shredded wheat	½ cup
Sugar-frosted cereal	½ cup
Wheat germ	3 tablespoons

Starchy Vegetables

Food Item	Serving Size
Baked beans	⅓ cup
Corn kernels	½ cup
Corn on cob, large	½ cob (5 ounces)
Mixed vegetables with corn, peas, or pasta	1 cup
Peas, green	½ cup
Plantain	½ cup
Potato, boiled	½ cup or ½ medium (3 ounces)
Potato, baked with skin	¼ large (3 ounces)
Potato, mashed	½ cup
Squash, winter (acorn, butternut, pumpkin)	1 cup
Sweet potato or yam, plain	½ cup

Crackers and Snacks

Food Item	Serving Size
Animal crackers	8
Graham cracker, 2½-inch square	3
Matzo	¾ ounce
Melba toast	4 slices
Oyster crackers	24
Popcorn, popped, no fat added, or low-fat microwave	3 cups
Pretzels	¾ ounce
Rice cakes, 4 inches across	2
Saltine-type crackers	6
Snack chips, fat-free or baked (tortilla, potato)	15–20 (¾ ounce)
Whole-wheat crackers, no fat added	2–5 (¾ ounce)

Beans, Peas, and Lentils*

Food Item	Serving Size
Beans and peas (garbanzo, pinto, kidney, white, split, black-eyed)	½ cup
Lentils	½ cup
Lima beans	⅔ cup
Miso†	3 tablespoons

*Count as 1 starch exchange plus 1 very lean meat exchange.
†Contains 400 mg or more sodium per exchange.

Starchy Foods Prepared with Fat*

Food Item	Serving Size
Biscuit, 1½ inches across	1
Chow mein noodles	½ cup
Corn bread, 2-inch cube	1 (2 ounces)
Crackers, round butter type	6
Croutons	1 cup
French-fried potatoes (oven-baked)	1 cup (2 ounces)

continued

Starchy Foods Prepared with Fat, *continued**

Food Item	Serving Size
Granola	¼ cup
Hummus	⅓ cup
Muffin, 5 ounces	⅕ (1 ounce)
Popcorn, microwaved	3 cups
Sandwich crackers, cheese or peanut butter filling	3
Snack chips (potato, tortilla)	9–13 (¾ ounce)
Stuffing, bread (prepared)	⅓ cup
Taco shell, 6 inches across	2
Waffle, 4 inches across	1
Whole wheat crackers, fat added	4–6 (1 ounce)

*Count as 1 starch exchange plus 1 fat exchange.

Fruit

Each food in the fruit list contains about 15 grams of carbohydrates and 60 calories per serving. One fruit exchange is equivalent to one of the following servings:

- 1 small fresh fruit (4 ounces)
- ½ cup canned or fresh fruit or unsweetened fruit juice
- ¼ cup dried fruit

Fruit

Food Item	Serving Size
Apple, unpeeled, small	1 (4 ounces)
Applesauce, unsweetened	½ cup
Apples, dried	4 rings
Apricots, fresh	4 whole (5½ ounces)
Apricots, dried	8 halves
Apricots, canned	½ cup
Banana, small	1 (4 ounces)

Fruit, *continued*

Food Item	Serving Size
Blackberries	¾ cup
Blueberries	¾ cup
Cantaloupe, small	⅓ melon (11 ounces) or 1 cup cubes
Cherries, sweet, fresh	12 (3 ounces)
Cherries, sweet, canned	½ cup
Dates	3
Figs, fresh	1½ large or 2 medium (3½ ounces)
Figs, dried	1½
Fruit cocktail	½ cup
Grapefruit, large	½ (11 ounces)
Grapefruit sections, canned	¾ cup
Grapes, small	17 (3 ounces)
Honeydew melon	1 slice (10 ounces) or 1 cup cubes
Kiwi	1 (3½ ounces)
Mandarin oranges, canned	¾ cup
Mango, small	½ fruit (5½ ounces) or ½ cup
Nectarine, small	1 (5 ounces)
Orange, small	1 (6½ ounces)
Papaya	½ fruit (8 ounces) or 1 cup cubes
Peach, medium, fresh	1 (4 ounces)
Peaches, canned	½ cup
Pear, large, fresh	½ (4 ounces)
Pears, canned	½ cup
Pineapple, fresh	¾ cup
Pineapple, canned	½ cup
Plums, small	2 (5 ounces)
Plums, canned	½ cup
Plums, dried (prunes)	3
Raisins	2 tablespoons
Raspberries	1 cup
Strawberries	1¼ cups whole berries
Tangerines, small	2 (8 ounces)
Watermelon	1 slice (13½ ounces) or 1¼ cups cubes

Fruit Juice, Unsweetened

Food Item	Serving Size
Apple juice or cider	½ cup
Cranberry juice cocktail	⅓ cup
Cranberry juice cocktail, reduced-calorie	1 cup
Fruit juice blends, 100% juice	⅓ cup
Grape juice	⅓ cup
Grapefruit juice	½ cup
Orange juice	½ cup
Pineapple juice	½ cup
Prune juice	⅓ cup

Milk

Each serving of milk or milk product in the following list contains about 12 grams of carbohydrates and 8 grams of protein. The amount of fat in the milk (up to 8 grams per serving) determines whether it is identified as skim/very low fat milk, low-fat milk, or whole milk. In general, one milk exchange is 1 cup.

Fat-Free and Low-Fat Milk (0–3 grams fat per serving)

Food Item	Serving Size
Fat-free milk	1 cup
½% milk	1 cup
1% milk	1 cup
Buttermilk, low-fat or fat-free	1 cup
Evaporated fat-free milk	½ cup
Fat-free dry milk	⅓ cup dry
Soy milk, low-fat or fat-free	1 cup
Yogurt, fat-free, flavored, sweetened with nonnutritive sweetener and fructose	⅔ cup (6 ounces)
Yogurt, plain, fat-free	⅔ cup (6 ounces)

Reduced-Fat (5 grams fat per serving)

Food Item	Serving Size
2% milk	1 cup
Soy milk	1 cup
Sweet acidophilus milk	1 cup
Yogurt, plain, low-fat	¾ cup

Whole Milk (8 grams fat per serving)

Food Item	Serving Size
Whole milk	1 cup
Evaporated whole milk	½ cup
Goat's milk	1 cup
Kefir	1 cup
Yogurt, plain (made from whole milk)	¾ cup

Sweets, Desserts, and Other Carbohydrates

The exchange equivalencies and servings for this category vary depending on the food in question.

Sweets, Desserts, and Other Carbohydrates

Food Item	Serving Size	Exchanges per Serving
Angel food cake, unfrosted	¹⁄₁₂ cake (about 2 ounces)	2 carbohydrates
Brownie, small, unfrosted	2-inch square (about 1 ounce)	1 carbohydrate, 1 fat
Cake, unfrosted	2-inch square (about 1 ounce)	1 carbohydrate, 1 fat
Cake, frosted	2-inch square (about 2 ounces)	2 carbohydrates, 1 fat

continued

Sweets, Desserts, and Other Carbohydrates, *continued*

Food Item	Serving Size	Exchanges per Serving
Cookie or sandwich cookie with creme filling	2 small (about ⅔ ounce)	1 carbohydrate, 1 fat
Cookies, sugar-free	3 small or 1 large (¾–1 ounce)	1 carbohydrate, 1–2 fats
Cranberry sauce, jellied	¼ cup	1½ carbohydrates
Cupcake, frosted	1 small (about 2 ounces)	2 carbohydrates, 1 fat
Doughnut, plain cake	1 medium (1½ ounces)	1½ carbohydrates, 2 fats
Doughnut, glazed	3¾ inches across (2 ounces)	2 carbohydrates, 2 fats
Energy, sport, or breakfast bar	1 bar (1⅓ ounces)	1½ carbohydrates, 0–1 fat
Energy, sport, or breakfast bar	1 bar (2 ounces)	2 carbohydrates, 1 fat
Fruit cobbler	½ cup (3½ ounces)	3 carbohydrates, 1 fat
Fruit juice bars, frozen, 100% juice	1 bar (3 ounces)	1 carbohydrate
Fruit snacks, chewy (pureed fruit concentrate)	1 roll (¾ ounce)	1 carbohydrate
Fruit spreads, 100% fruit	1½ tablespoons	1 carbohydrate
Gelatin, regular	½ cup	1 carbohydrate
Gingersnaps	3	1 carbohydrate
Granola or snack bar, regular or low-fat	1 bar (1 ounce)	1½ carbohydrates
Honey	1 tablespoon	1 carbohydrate
Ice cream	½ cup	1 carbohydrate, 2 fats
Ice cream, light	½ cup	1 carbohydrate, 1 fat
Ice cream, low-fat	½ cup	1½ carbohydrates
Ice cream, fat-free, no sugar added	½ cup	1 carbohydrate
Jam or jelly, regular	1 tablespoon	1 carbohydrate
Milk, chocolate, whole	1 cup	2 carbohydrates, 1 fat
Pie, fruit, 2 crusts	⅙ of 8-inch commercially prepared pie	3 carbohydrates, 2 fats
Pie, pumpkin or custard	⅛ of 8-inch commercially prepared pie	2 carbohydrates, 2 fats
Pudding, regular (made with reduced-fat milk)	½ cup	2 carbohydrates

Sweets, Desserts, and Other Carbohydrates, *continued*

Food Item	Serving Size	Exchanges per Serving
Pudding, sugar-free or sugar- and fat-free (made with fat-free milk)	½ cup	1 carbohydrate
Reduced-calorie meal replacement (shake)	1 can (10–11 ounces)	1½ carbohydrates, 0–1 fat
Rice milk, low-fat or fat-free, plain	1 cup	1 carbohydrate
Rice milk, low-fat, flavored	1 cup	1½ carbohydrates
Salad dressing, fat-free	¼ cup	1 carbohydrate
Sherbet or sorbet	½ cup	2 carbohydrates
Spaghetti sauce or pasta sauce, canned	½ cup	1 carbohydrate, 1 fat
Sports drink	8 ounces (1 cup)	1 carbohydrate
Sugar	1 tablespoon	1 carbohydrate
Sweet roll or Danish	1 (2½ ounces)	2½ carbohydrates, 2 fats
Syrup, light	2 tablespoons	1 carbohydrate
Syrup, regular	1 tablespoon	1 carbohydrate
Syrup, regular	¼ cup	4 carbohydrates
Vanilla wafers	5	1 carbohydrate, 1 fat
Yogurt, frozen	½ cup	1 carbohydrate, 0–1 fat
Yogurt, frozen, fat-free	⅓ cup	1 carbohydrate
Yogurt, low-fat with fruit	1 cup	0–1 fat

Nonstarchy Vegetables

One vegetable exchange contains about 5 grams of carbohydrates, 2 grams of protein, 0 grams of fat, and 25 calories per serving. In general, one vegetable exchange is equivalent to one of the following servings:

- ½ cup cooked vegetables or vegetable juice
- 1 cup raw vegetables

Artichoke

Artichoke hearts

Asparagus

Beans (green, wax, Italian)

Bean sprouts

Beets

Broccoli

Brussels spouts

Cabbage

Carrots

Cauliflower

Celery

Cucumber

Eggplant

Green onions or scallions

Greens (collard, kale,
  mustard, turnip)

Kohlrabi

Leeks

Mixed vegetables (without
  corn, peas, or pasta)

Mushrooms

Okra

Onions

Peppers (all varieties)

Radishes

Salad greens (endive, escarole,
  lettuce, romaine, spinach)

Sauerkraut

Snow peas

Spinach

Summer squash

Tomato

Tomatoes, canned

Tomato sauce

Tomato/vegetable juice

Turnips

Water chestnuts

Watercress

Zucchini

Meat and Meat Substitutes

Meat and meat substitutes contain both protein and fat. Based on the fat they contain, meats are divided into four lists:

- Very lean meat and substitutes contain about 7 grams of protein, up to 1 gram of fat, and 35 calories per serving.
- Lean meat and substitutes contain about 7 grams of protein, 3 grams of fat, and 55 calories per serving.

- Medium-fat meat and substitutes contain about 7 grams of protein, 5 grams of fat, and 75 calories per serving.
- High-fat meat and substitutes contain 7 grams of protein, 8 grams of fat, and 100 calories per serving.

In general, one meat exchange is equivalent to one of the following servings:

- 1 ounce meat, fish, poultry, or cheese
- ½ cup beans, peas, or lentils

Very Lean Meat and Substitutes

Food Item	Serving Size
Poultry	
Chicken or turkey (white meat, no skin), Cornish hen (no skin)	1 ounce
Fish	
Fresh or frozen cod, flounder, haddock, halibut, trout, lox (smoked salmon); tuna, fresh or canned in water	1 ounce
Shellfish	
Clams, crab, lobster, scallops, shrimp, imitation shellfish	1 ounce
Game	
Duck or pheasant (no skin), venison, buffalo, ostrich	1 ounce
Cheese with up to 1 gram of fat per ounce	
Fat-free or low-fat cottage cheese	¼ cup
Fat-free cheese	1 ounce
Other	
Processed sandwich meats with up to 1 gram of fat per ounce (deli thin, shaved meats, chipped beef, turkey ham)	1 ounce
Beans, peas, lentils (cooked)*	½ cup
Egg whites	2

continued

Very Lean Meat and Substitutes, *continued*

Food Item	Serving Size
Egg substitutes, plain	¼ cup
Hot dogs with up to 1 gram of fat per ounce	1 ounce
Kidney (high in cholesterol)	1 ounce
Sausage with up to 1 gram of fat per ounce	1 ounce

*Count as 1 very lean meat plus 1 starch exchange.

Lean Meat and Substitutes

Food Item	Serving Size
Beef	
USDA Select or Choice grades of lean beef trimmed of fat, such as round, sirloin, and flank steak; tenderloin; roast (rib, chuck, rump); steak (T-bone, porterhouse, cube); ground round	1 ounce
Pork	
Lean pork, such as fresh ham; canned, cured, or boiled ham; Canadian bacon; tenderloin; center loin chop	1 ounce
Lamb	
Roast, chop, or leg	1 ounce
Veal	
Lean chop, roast	1 ounce
Poultry	
Chicken or turkey (dark meat, no skin), chicken (white meat, with skin), domestic duck or goose (well drained of fat, no skin)	1 ounce
Fish	
Herring (uncreamed or smoked)	1 ounce
Oysters	6 medium
Salmon (fresh or canned), catfish	1 ounce
Sardines (canned)	2 medium
Tuna (canned in oil, drained)	1 ounce

Lean Meat and Substitutes, *continued*

Food Item	Serving Size
Game	
Goose (no skin) or rabbit	1 ounce
Cheese	
4.5% fat cottage cheese	¼ cup
Grated Parmesan	2 tablespoons
Cheese with 1–3 grams of fat per ounce	1 ounce
Other	
Hot dogs with 1–3 grams of fat per ounce	1½ ounces
Processed sandwich meat with 1–3 grams of fat per ounce (turkey pastrami, kielbasa)	1 ounce
Liver, heart (high in cholesterol)	1 ounce

Medium-Fat Meat and Substitutes

Food Item	Serving Size
Beef	
Most beef products (ground beef, meat loaf, corned beef, short ribs, Prime grades of meat trimmed of fat, such as prime rib)	1 ounce
Pork	
Top loin, chop, Boston butt, cutlet	1 ounce
Lamb	
Rib roast, ground	1 ounce
Veal	
Cutlet (ground or cubed, unbreaded)	1 ounce
Poultry	
Chicken (dark meat, with skin), ground turkey or ground chicken, fried chicken (with skin)	1 ounce

continued

Medium-Fat Meat and Substitutes, *continued*

Food Item	Serving Size
Fish	
Any fried fish product	1 ounce
Cheese with 3–5 grams fat per ounce	
Feta	1 ounce
Mozzarella	1 ounce
Ricotta	¼ cup (2 ounces)
Other	
Egg (high in cholesterol, limit to 3 per week)	1
Sausage with 3–5 grams of fat per ounce	1 ounce
Tempeh	¼ cup
Tofu	4 ounces or ½ cup

High-Fat Meat and Substitutes*

Food Item	Serving Size
Pork	
Spareribs, ground pork, pork sausage	1 ounce
Cheese	
All regular cheeses, such as American, cheddar, Monterey Jack, Swiss	1 ounce
Other	
Bacon	3 slices (20 slices/pound)
Hot dog (turkey or chicken)	1 (10/pound)
Hot dog (beef, pork, or combination)[†]	1 (10/pound)
Processed sandwich meats with 5–8 grams of fat per ounce, such as bologna, pimiento loaf, salami	1 ounce
Sausage, such as bratwurst, Italian, knockwurst, Polish (smoked)	1 ounce
Peanut butter (contains unsaturated fat)	1 tablespoon

*Remember, these items are high in saturated fat, cholesterol, and calories and may raise blood cholesterol levels if eaten regularly.

†Count as 1 high-fat meat plus 1 fat exchange.

Fats

Fats are divided into three groups based on the main type of fat they contain—polyunsaturated, monounsaturated, and saturated. One fat exchange contains about 5 grams of fat and 45 calories. In general, one fat exchange is equivalent to one of the following servings:

- 1 teaspoon regular margarine or vegetable oil
- 1 tablespoon regular salad dressing

Polyunsaturated Fats

Food Item	Serving Size
Margarine (stick, tub, or squeeze)	1 teaspoon
Margarine, lower-fat spread (30%–50% vegetable oil)	1 tablespoon
Mayonnaise, regular	1 teaspoon
Mayonnaise, reduced-fat	1 tablespoon
Miracle Whip salad dressing, regular	2 teaspoons
Miracle Whip salad dressing, reduced-fat	1 tablespoon
Nuts (walnuts, English)	4 halves
Oil (corn, safflower, soybean)	1 teaspoon
Salad dressing, regular	1 tablespoon
Salad dressing, reduced-fat	2 tablespoons
Seeds (pumpkin, sunflower)	1 tablespoon

Monounsaturated Fats

Food Item	Serving Size
Avocado, medium	2 tablespoons (1 ounce)
Nuts (almonds, cashews)	6 nuts
Nuts, mixed (50% peanuts)	6 nuts
Nuts (pecans)	4 halves
Oil (canola, olive, peanut)	1 teaspoon
Olives, ripe (black)	8 large
Olives, green, stuffed	10 large

continued

Monounsaturated Fats, *continued*

Food Item	Serving Size
Peanuts	10 nuts
Peanut butter, smooth or crunchy	½ tablespoon
Sesame seeds	1 tablespoon
Tahini or sesame paste	2 teaspoons

Saturated Fats

Food Item	Serving Size
Bacon, cooked	1 slice (20 slices/pound)
Bacon grease	1 teaspoon
Butter, stick	1 teaspoon
Butter, whipped	2 teaspoons
Butter, reduced-fat	1 tablespoon
Chitterlings, boiled	2 tablespoons (½ ounce)
Coconut, sweetened, shredded	2 tablespoons
Coconut milk	1 tablespoon
Cream, half-and-half	2 tablespoons
Cream cheese, regular	1 tablespoon (½ ounce)
Cream cheese, reduced-fat	1½ tablespoons (¾ ounce)
Shortening or lard	1 teaspoon
Sour cream, regular	2 tablespoons
Sour cream, reduced-fat	3 tablespoons

Free Foods

A *free food* is any food or drink that contains less than 20 calories or less than or equal to 5 grams of carbohydrates per serving. Limit foods with a serving size to three servings per day. Be sure to spread them throughout the day. Eating all three servings at one time could raise your blood glucose level. Foods listed without a serving size can be eaten whenever you like.

Fat-Free or Reduced-Fat Foods

Food Item	Serving Size*
Cream cheese, fat-free	1 tablespoon (½ ounce)
Creamers, nondairy, liquid	1 tablespoon
Creamers, nondairy, powdered	2 teaspoons
Mayonnaise, fat-free	1 tablespoon
Mayonnaise, reduced-fat	1 teaspoon
Margarine spread, fat-free	4 tablespoons
Margarine spread, reduced-fat	1 teaspoon
Miracle Whip salad dressing, fat-free	1 tablespoon
Miracle Whip salad dressing, reduced-fat	1 teaspoon
Nonstick cooking spray	
Salad dressing, fat-free or low-fat	1 tablespoon
Salad dressing, fat-free, Italian	2 tablespoons
Sour cream, fat-free or reduced-fat	1 tablespoon
Whipped topping, regular	1 tablespoon
Whipped topping, light or fat-free	2 tablespoons

*Foods listed without a serving size can be eaten whenever you like.

Sugar-Free Foods

Food Item	Serving Size*
Candy, hard, sugar-free	1 candy
Gelatin dessert, sugar-free	
Gelatin, unflavored	
Gum, sugar-free	
Jam or jelly, light	2 teaspoons
Sugar substitutes[†]	
Syrup, sugar-free	2 tablespoons

*Foods listed without a serving size can be eaten whenever you like.

[†]Sugar substitutes, alternatives, or replacements that are approved by the Food and Drug Administration (FDA) are safe to use. Common brand names include Equal (aspartame), Splenda (sucralose), Sprinkle Sweet (saccharin), SugarTwin (saccharin), Sweet One (acesulfame-K), Sweet-10 (saccharin), and Sweet'n Low (saccharin).

Drinks

Food Item	Serving Size*
Bouillon, broth, consomme	
Bouillon or broth, low-sodium	
Carbonated or mineral water	
Club soda	
Cocoa powder, unsweetened	1 tablespoon
Coffee	
Diet soft drinks, sugar-free	
Drink mixes, sugar-free	
Tea	
Tonic water, sugar-free	

*Beverages listed without a serving size can be drunk whenever you like.

Condiments

Food Item	Serving Size*
Horseradish	
Ketchup	1 tablespoon
Lemon juice	
Lime juice	
Mustard	
Pickle relish	1 tablespoon
Pickles, dill	1½ medium
Pickles, sweet (bread and butter)	2 slices
Pickles, sweet (gherkin)	¾ ounce
Salsa	¼ cup
Soy sauce, regular or light	1 tablespoon
Taco sauce	1 tablespoon
Vinegar	
Yogurt	2 tablespoons

*Condiments listed without a serving size can be used whenever you like.

Seasonings*

Food Item	Serving Size†
Flavoring extracts	
Garlic	
Herbs, fresh or dried	
Pimiento	
Spices	
Tabasco or hot pepper sauce	
Wine, used in cooking	
Worcestershire sauce	

*Be careful with seasonings that contain sodium or are salts, such as garlic or celery salt and lemon pepper.
†Seasonings listed without a serving size can be used whenever you like.

Combination Foods

Many of the foods we eat are mixed together in various combinations. These combination foods do not fit into any one exchange list. Often it is hard to tell what is in a casserole dish or prepared food item. This is a list of exchanges for some typical combination foods. This list will help you fit these foods into your meal plan. Ask your dietitian for information about any other combination foods you would like to eat.

Combination Foods

Food	Serving Size	Exchanges per Serving
Entrees		
Tuna-noodle casserole, lasagna, spaghetti with meatballs, chili with beans, or macaroni and cheese	1 cup (8 ounces)	2 carbohydrates, 2 medium-fat meats
Chow mein (without noodles or rice)	2 cups (16 ounces)	1 carbohydrate, 2 lean meats
Tuna or chicken salad	1/2 cup (3 1/2 ounces)	1/2 carbohydrate, 2 lean meats, 1 fat
Frozen Entrees and Meals		
Dinner-type meal	14–17 ounces	3 carbohydrates, 3 medium-fat meats, 3 fats
Meatless burger, soy based	3 ounces	1/2 carbohydrate, 2 lean meats
Meatless burger, vegetable and starch based	3 ounces	1 carbohydrate, 1 lean meat
Pizza, cheese, thin crust	1/4 of 12-inch (6 ounces)	2 carbohydrates, 2 medium-fat meats, 1 fat
Pizza, meat topping, thin crust	1/4 of 12-inch (6 ounces)	2 carbohydrates, 2 medium-fat meats, 2 fats
Pot pie	1 (7 ounces)	2 1/2 carbohydrates, 1 medium-fat meat, 3 fats
Entree or meal with less than 340 calories	About 8–11 ounces	2–3 carbohydrates, 1–2 lean meats
Soups		
Bean	1 cup	1 carbohydrate, 1 very lean meat
Cream (made with water)	1 cup (8 ounces)	1 carbohydrate, 1 fat
Instant	6 ounces prepared	1 carbohydrate
Instant with beans or lentils	8 ounces prepared	2 1/2 carbohydrates, 1 very lean meat
Split pea (made with water)	1/2 cup (4 ounces)	1 carbohydrate
Tomato (made with water)	1 cup (8 ounces)	1 carbohydrate
Vegetable beef, chicken noodle, or other broth type	1 cup (8 ounces)	1 carbohydrate

Index